Find **Joy** in the **Middle**

James Hempsall

BIS Publishers

BIS PUBLISHERS

BIS Publishers
Timorplein 46
1094 CC Amsterdam
The Netherlands
bis@bispublishers.com
www.bispublishers.com
ISBN 978 90 636 9846 1
Copyright © 2025 James Hempsall and BIS Publishers.

OUT-RUNNER

Design by Rich Cowan / Outrunner
rich@outrunner.co.uk
+44 (0) 7765957217

You will discover yourself in the middle at least once. Whether it be in middle age, by being a middle child, finding yourself in middle management, being middle class, or occupying a middle ground or place.

The trouble is people have negative thoughts about things in the middle, and some even ridicule it. We are very often told it is not something to aim for, nor a good place to be in.

There is a risk of languishing in the middle, which means being stuck in a state of apathy or stagnation. This can be a place where you're experiencing significant happiness or sadness, and feeling all the effects of boredom or lack of meaning.

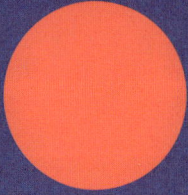

So...

Look again at the middle. When you find yourself there (because you will), or you feel confused, underwhelmed or disappointed by it (because you might), this book will help you to understand, embrace and celebrate it (because you really should make the most of all middles).

We have a problem to solve.

The middle affects us all, yet it is mostly described in derogatory and unhelpful terms. At best, the middle is overlooked, at worst we are fed misinformation, and loaded with lots of unhelpful stuff. On the bookshelves there are silly books and mocking magazine articles and greeting cards poking fun at the middle aged. In comedy clubs, stand-ups use middle themes as rich laughter-fodder. That results in too many of us believing the middle is bad, unattractive, disappointing, a figure of fun, ridiculous, or embarrassing. This is strange as middles pervade all facets of life and work.

I say, don't accept this. It is plainly and simply unfair that things are this way. It is a shame the middle hasn't been better described or valued before. The middle is not mediocre, it is something to love, aim for, be at peace with, and ultimately be happier in. We have the opportunity to do something about this.

This is a book for everyone.

Find Joy in the Middle is a book for those who become middle children, and their siblings, parents, friends, or work colleagues. It is for anyone interested in society's constructs (class in other words), especially the middle classes. It is for anyone who will be middle aged in the future, is middle aged now, and those who can look back and reflect upon their middle age. It is for people who work in middle management, underneath or above it, and those who lead or manage it. It is for anyone thinking about occupying the middle ground in opinions or views. And it is for anyone helping other people to come to terms with their own middle. That means this is a book for everyone.

I don't think we are talking about all things middle anywhere near usefully or positively enough. I want you to deliberately, consciously, and positively place the middle firmly in your sights, targets, aims, or goals.

The middle is something to be interested in.

You may have bought this book because you are curious or identify as one or more of the middles. It may have been a gift from a friend who thinks you may be interested. You might be thinking about going straight to the chapter you most relate to first. Indeed, I invite you to do just that. Let me tell you though, there's plenty of intersectionality to be considered here, things like how middle children behave at work, especially in middle management,

how the middle aged are situated at work (or not), and how all the middles affect how we occupy the middle ground or place in social groupings and behaviours.

The middle really is a special place that has so much more to offer than merely being between other things. Find Joy in the Middle is part self-help, part popular science or psychology, part opinion-piece, part parenting manual, part philosophy, and part business guide. All those parts invite you to unlearn everything you've been told so far, because I believe there is much more joy and happiness to be discovered than we are led to believe.

The middle is a fact of life your parents, your friends and family, or even your boss ought to have told you about. If they haven't, then you will want to read this book. Maybe they could read it too.

——o——

Thank you.

Thank you to the friends and colleagues who have shared experiences and observations, and listened to me when I was developing these ideas and who have contributed and shaped them or allowed me to observe discreetly – whether you knew you were doing that or not.

I appreciate the time some of you spent reading chapters, or let me read them to you, and for sharing your reactions, comments, edits, and reviews. And thank you to those of you who I interviewed so I could better understand your lived experiences in the middle. You've all made this book much better than it would've been if I had written it alone. For all of that I am truly lucky and very grateful.

Let's hope the result is that more people will
Find Joy in the Middle.

What's Inside?

All about the middle

Having occupied myself thinking about the middle over the last few years, I have found it to be typically defined by what it is not, the space, place, or thing between others. It is not the richest or the poorest, not the beginning or the end, not north or south or east or west, not the best or the worst, not the left or the right, not black or white, and it cannot ever be the youngest or the oldest. The middle isn't a place or a destination, neither is it boastful or showy, edgy or risky, different or extreme. It doesn't naturally brag or shout about itself, instead it is gloriously modest and reserved.

We all seem to know what it isn't. What's missing is any real consensus of what it *is*. Something compounded by the struggles we may have with terms like, in-between, comfortable, modest, stuck in the middle, the middle of nowhere, okay, reasonable, or grey. None of these terms are linked to thrilling concepts, are they?

The word middle is a common and regular feature of our modern language. Phrases and terms like 'middle of the road', 'stuck in the middle', 'middle England', 'middle America', 'middle ages', and 'middleman', amongst very many others, are all extremely familiar to us. We often use them carelessly and unthinkingly. What at first glance appears to be an innocuous term is a much more complex concept than we might have first imagined.

It seems that middles don't always enjoy the glamour, the success, or the attention that the top or the best basks in. Instead, the middle is somewhere between success and failure. This position may come from a lack ambition, or not achieving what people consider to be the very best or choosing the peace of an inconspicuous or easier life. That means people can be hesitant about what to say; 'congratulations' seems too much, 'never mind' appears a little rude. This can cause us to not talk about it often, to overlook it, or misunderstand or undervalue the middle.

That can cause us to travel through it without noticing or conscious thought, and if we do wake up and find ourselves in the middle we can feel a sense of confusion or disappointment.

People can feel uneasy and be preoccupied about how they fit into family or work hierarchies. They can be anxious about their middle age. They can be embarrassed, in denial, or graspingly aspirational about their middle classness. The middle at work can be an absolute nightmare if you are in it (and I have been), if you are either side of it (again been there and done that), or if you rely upon it either as a boss or a worker (got the T shirt). We may feel apologetic or embarrassed about holding middle ground views, especially in these synthetically polarised times, when we are supposed to be of one mind or the other. There is also the risk we seek out those echo chambers where we find people like us, people who agree with us, and don't have the benefit of being with others who hold diverse views and opinions.

To cope, we either ignore it, sneer at it, judge it, deny it, or we use humour to defend or distract from our confusion and embarrassment. I think we could be much more prepared to celebrate and enjoy the middle, without embarrassment or apology, but with joy instead. There are positives, the middle offers the place for sanctuary, peace, or harmony.

I don't want us to be discombobulated or disillusioned. Instead, I want us to be much happier in the middle. To do that, we need to better appreciate it and to understand its unique qualities and features more fully.

Society has conspired against it.

I think the middle has been subjected to orchestrated and sustained attacks for centuries. It has been shaped by societal trends and manipulated by those in positions of power. The history books, writers, moviemakers, media moguls, marketeers, advertisers, social media platforms, and other aspects of life (modern and in the past) have all combined to create a grand illusion. They all want us to feel bad, disappointed, or unfulfilled about the middle, to judge it, reject it, or to swerve or avoid it. Why might they do that? Is it to make these plotters feel better about themselves, or to feel more successful at the expense of others by layering on these feelings of latent dissatisfaction? Presumably this all gives them something, somewhere, or somebody to look down upon, to control, to sell to, and to further influence for their own advantage. I venture these behaviours are motivated and informed by a sense of lacking in themselves or palpable fear of anything different to their own lived experience or their version of convenient truth. I am pretty sure of that. The middle needs a rebrand, and that is what I am setting out to do.

History is imperfect.

To gain some insight into why all this may have happened, I want us to go back in time. Because much of what we think about the middle has its roots in history. We can learn from the distant and recent past as it helps us to understand the journey made so far, and to ponder the one yet to come. This, you shall come to realise, is a common feature of getting to grips with middles; as we look up and down, left and right, back and forth.

French statesman, Napoleon Bonaparte said history *"is the version of past events that people have decided to agree upon"*. It is edited to suit the convenience of the storyteller, cultural construct, legislature, powerbase, religion, and society. We have all fallen victim for too long to the construct of small groups of men, with narrow criteria, deciding what is worthy or historical. I think it was the English statesman, Sir Winston Churchill who said *"History is written by the winners"*, others have repeated such sage advice, and I absolutely agree! These winners are those who survived battles and wars, won political or religious positions, held resources or social status, or did well in education, in exams, or on school sports day. It explains why so much of our currency, postage stamps, art works, building names, schools, and the like is decorated by or named after white, able bodied, males. It also explains why

"History is written by the winners."

———○———

Sir Winston Churchill

disproportionate value is placed upon people that got the distinctions, the awards, and the medals.

People still delete the history they don't want others to read. Just check their internet browser for an example of how diligent they can be. It is typically the tidiest and thing on people's desktops. Trouble is too many people use history as a defence, and as a reason or justification not to change. They say things have always been this way or that way. And there's no need to do things any differently. If it isn't broken, don't fix it – they say. That's a big problem when we're thinking about subjectivity and the writing of (in)accurate history. People start to believe that everything and anything is controlled by others in power, and not by the rest of us. All of this simply dances to the tune of those orchestrating it, we worry about the things they tell us we should be scared of. And in the case of middle things, that hasn't been beneficial at all. We will discover later how available facts, our personal subjectivity, and the perceptions of others, get in the way of the middle, but they can also unlock our truths. These are huge factors in how the middle is defined and understood – especially for class, age, and the middle ground or place.

The Middle Ages.

Let's first consider the Middle Ages, a period starting around 500 until approximately 1,500 CE. It was a time also known as the 'dark ages'. As you might have already noticed, versions of history have the capacity to make us feel nervous about the middle. This is important. The tone and terminology are deliberately designed to create fear of what we might discover in the 'dark'. It is a tried and tested method, attributing colour to reinforce and control our thoughts and feelings about things, or a particular episode or era. Such methods remain endemic, they are powerfully and depressingly present in current society, and in bias and discrimination.

Back to the case in point, fundamentally we need to ask why the middle ages were called that in the first place. And who decided and when. The period was defined by political turmoil and social unrest that resulted in many wars and battles. There was much disease, plague, and famine which meant millions of Europeans were ill, close to death, or they died.

Infant mortality rates were so high (estimated at 20-30%) they decreased the average lifespan to 45 years, which by today's measures is arguably in the middle aged ballpark, or at least in the margins of it (for most at least). Others have even postulated life expectancy may have been as low as 30 back then. People did live through their own middle age and into old age, if they manage to navigate the perils of childhood.

There was lots of change in Europe at this time. It was a period of about 1,000 years between the fall of the Imperial Roman Empire and the early beginnings of the modern Europe we know today. It predated the discoveries and developments of what Europeans have come to call 'the New World'. A world not new to the indigenous people already freely living undisturbed and unexploited in it, I might add. This was also known as the Medieval Age (a translation of the Latin Medium Aevum). It was term ostensibly prompted by a real sense of loss when the societal order, knowledge, and technological advances of the Roman Empire were being quickly forgotten. With ensuing invasions of Barbarian tribes, mass population migrations, devastation to communities and social disarray, life was doubly hard and all too brief. People then didn't have much time or opportunity to think about being middle aged, they simply didn't live long enough. Middle age angst was most likely not an issue, the population had their basic survival at front of mind. Birth order I would suggest wasn't such a concern either as the structure of families was far too fluid and unreliable. Class structures were evident though. The uppers consisted of royalty, the clergy, and nobility, while the middles were professionals, soldiers or merchants, and the lowers were the serfs and peasants.

Because the middle ages were the time between the better Roman and arguably advanced modern times, the middle, as a result, became a term that meant we weren't quite as bright or civilised, clean or healthy, scientific or mathematic as the Greek or Roman societies. It was generally considered a 'backwards time in human history'. So, there we have it, evidence the middle has been tainted with historical and entrenched values and negativity for centuries. It's not just middle, it is dark. It is not forward it is backward. It is just not as easy or safe. All that baggage and bias surely takes quite a while to shake off. The middle ages were characterised more by what they were not, than what they were, something that has continued to be a common feature of all types of middle.

The modern ages.

Middles still sit awkwardly with modern life, and that's not just a problem, it feels like sedition. Society has tended to weaponise the middle. You might have had a terrible, confusing and tension-filled time being a middle child – with the (un)wanted attention of your siblings or parents. Friends and family may have mocked you for middle class pretentions or characteristics. If you are of a certain age, you have most likely been teased for being middle aged – behaving like it, or appearing to approach it either too soon, or in various telling ways, or indeed being in denial about it (if you've not got there yet, you have got that to look forward to). You will remember the words said, the giggles, the sideways glances, or the 'humorous' birthday cards received. You may have been sneered at for having middle views or politics, or accused of being undecided, sitting on the fence, or being dispassionate, or of holding insufficiently strong or passionate opinions. You may have noticed judgement if you live, or occupy another space, in the middle. Somewhere that isn't in the cut and thrust of those glamorously edgy margins.

This is all a real pity; it is a scandal. To be happy about your journey so far, where you find yourself now, or where you are travelling to, is something to value and to consciously consider. It is not something that should be used against you, either by you or others around you. This is your middle, your happiness, your plan.

On the shelf.

The authors of contemporary business books (not me obviously) have jumped on the bandwagon and are equally conspiratorial. There must be money in this. These books, you know, the ones that overcrowd the shelves of airport bookshops, are unashamedly macho, in the main. Like me, you have probably bought and read the same books on your holiday for as long as you can remember. Their titles are a reworking of familiar terms: power, effectiveness, goals, success, big, dreams, leadership, growth, acceleration, profit, riches, millionaire, billionaire, zillionaire – you get the drift. It's all the same words, just shuffled into a different order. You don't believe me? Visit any bookshop or scroll through online retailers and you will find them. Titles abound like 'Reach for the top', 'Be the best you can be', 'Live the dream'. They are written for the winners and the wannabees.

It seems anything short of aiming for the top, simply is just not good enough. There's very little mention of the middle, by that I mean anything other than the peaks they want us to aim for. Which by implication of its absence and exclusion is surely to be considered a failure by these authors. They instead attempt to persuade us greater success is within all of our reach, that we should be super-aspirational, and everything is possible (aspiration, we will learn later, is an important word when it comes to understanding the middle classes). They appear to believe that anything else just isn't good enough. Oh dear.

When it comes to self-help and the middle age in particular, then you will be reading themes that are less ambitious, with a focus on merely coping, inevitably experiencing crisis (especially for men), or the hazards of navigating crossroads.

It's an easy trap to fall into.

These promises, philosophies, and illusions are far too seductive. They are designed to be irresistible and addictive. It is easy to swallow the rhetoric and believe we must all dream big. I find them scary and coercive myself. Someone somewhere is trying to make us feel so inadequate that we follow the pursuits and activities of the aspirational. We are being told the top is best, and the bottom is the worst. The middle is nothing, invisible, or just not worthy. I aim to prove all of this wrong and offer new alternatives.

The trouble is, we start to internalise this nonsense, and imagine we could be a star, a superstar, a global celebrity – even a legend. We could be a brand this time next year (if prepared to wait so long), simply by virtue of goal-setting, sharing a well-timed and highly-stylised social media post, or spending the summer on TV, parading around swimwear in a holiday villa. It's the promise of an instant win, like the lottery sells us. You too can be famous, a success; it's such a toxic cocktail especially for our impressionable young people.

These temptations are setting up lots of people to fail, or at least feel a sense of failure, and that's worse. We really must do more to protect ourselves, and society as a whole (and the next generations for that matter) from such myths, delusions, and appallingly unhelpful influences. It is a huge mental health concern, research has shown social media decreases young people's self-esteem, and increases self-harm (including invasive cosmetic procedures), suicidal thoughts, and depression. By rejecting these deceptions and reducing their capacity to fuel our own self-sabotage and low self-esteem, we could find a better way – a middle way. Otherwise, we run the real risk of all this self-doubt, and feelings of inadequacy and disappointment lasting throughout lifetimes.

Fly me to the moon.

We, as a wider society, continue to tell children and young people the world is full of opportunity and dreams. We tell them life is the stuff of cartoon fairy tales, that handsome princes fall in love with lowly servants (at first sight), that beasts become beautiful, and that elephants can fly. The 'we' being parents and family members, teachers and mentors, the media, and more and more it's our politicians – who have decided to become interested in these matters. It is a well-intentioned message, in part. Why wouldn't we encourage our children to have dreams and goals? We all want the next generation to do better than ours, to break barriers, to be socially mobile, set new records and remove the shackles of society's limiting constructs. Surely it is all our job to show the next generation the horizon and give them the confidence to explore and/or go beyond it, through an authentic and well-informed lens?

I have tried to do my bit and perhaps made the mistakes of being too unrealistic myself. I remember once, when storytelling in a London primary school, telling a six-year-old girl, wearing silver trousers, that she could be an astronaut. She looked quizzically back, and I immediately feared the world had already made her believe such prospects were impossible. She didn't know anyone who was, or could be, an astronaut in her social world. She already believed that astronauts didn't come from Arsenal. Maybe I was being totally unrealistic and promoting unattainable goals. Perhaps I could have said she could work in a clothes shop – but that just perpetuates stereotypes and reinforces social immobility. My colleague giggled at me, rolling her eyes. I would like to imagine that child is now remembering that very moment whilst working on the International Space Station. Unlikely, I know. But she might just have taken that boost and used it to drive her through school. She might be working in a science lab right now. Fingers crossed she is doing something that is meaningful for her, and not sat alone contemplating her apparent failures. There is a real risk she is feeling a great sense of underachievement having not made the grade in science or at school. School may not have reached or connected with her, and her preferred learning style. She may be disaffected and disillusioned with what life has ended up being like. Because, unfortunately, opportunities like space travel and fairy tale dreams aren't in reach for most of us.

Instead, life gives us the hardest lessons. As we grow through childhood, adolescence and beyond, we collect different messages and realities. Our life-experiences teach us the best opportunities are mostly for those that already have been dealt a good hand of cards, or were born into the classes that have more and get more. This is one thing that stokes the fire of teenage anger and despair, and middle aged turning points (or so-called crises of confidence).

A matter of place.

Talking of where you are born and brought up, I should tell you I was born in the Midlands of England. I know from experience, the problems that arise from being a 'Midlander'. It's capitalised don't you know, which I think makes it all seem so much more important. Being in the Midlands, like all other types of middle is neither one nor the other. It isn't proper north, and it isn't proper south either. It's that space in between. A familiar tale, as I have frequently reminded you. My southern colleagues think I live *"up North"*, my northern colleagues think I live *"down South"*. The concept of the Midlands seems invariably misunderstood by pretty much all of them.

England isn't alone in its quandaries relating to middle locations. Middle America also gets a truly bad rap. It is the heartland of the mid-west between the east and the west coasts. The coasts being the home of the so-called metropolitan elite, the more 'sophisticated' states of the USA, they would have us believe. These coastal states cast judgements about middle America's perceived lack of culture, commonplace social characteristics, and political views that are considered to be ill-informed, simple, or just plain wrong, with a few exceptions.

Here is an example. In the US, the situation comedy called 'The Middle', the central character (Frankie) played by Patricia Heaton, was a middle aged, middle class mom struggling with keeping all the elements of her life together. Through her wit and good humour, she raised her family, whilst sadly lowering her expectations of life. They all lived in the fictional middle American town of Orson, Indiana. Frankie, we were shown, was tackling the mundane chaos of everyday life, along with husband Mike (who was adept at lurking in the side-lines of parenting). Frankie strived to bring up her three children, and hold down a less than successful job selling used cars. As she put it *"this is my life, it's not going to be in People Magazine or anything"*. There you have it, the sense of middling ordinariness and a lack of interesting star quality.

Not being on the cover of Time Magazine could be considered a good thing – couldn't it? Being normal looks much easier than standing out, being different, and receiving unwanted attention. Although I must admit, I might be tempted to accept the unlikely offer of a cover shoot, if one was made. But realistically and honestly, I consider privacy in the middle to be a wonderful and valuable thing.

Move away from a deficit model.

It is astonishing to me that we describe the middle in these deficit model terms. This just isn't doing anyone any good. It's much better to have a positive view, direction, and vision about most things and about the middle. I fear that if we don't find satisfactory and relevant understanding very soon, we might all suffer dire consequences and continue to be trapped in social quicksand. It will draw us in, pull us down, and sap our life force forever. Even worse, we may survive and be required to compromise all aspects of our lives and work instead. It is unfair that the middle is trapped into having to apologetically negotiate its position, in order to gain recognition, and inclusion. If you are a middle child or a middle manager, you will know exactly what I am talking about here.

Looking at five main middles.

There are lots of middles, and I've chosen five to explore in more detail. They relate to most of us, even if at first glance you may not think so, and I assure you there are lessons to be learned in all of them.

1. Class

I start with the idea of class, which situates us, our families and communities into an order of constructed society. A structure that seeks to determine, define, and limit (or at least manage) our behaviours, expectations, and opportunities. Class is designed to keep us in our place, or to label us, or to control our options and opportunities. At best it is used to understand how socially mobile, class-fluid, or successful we are.

Like it or not, society is still organised into various classes, inevitably the class in the middle is called just that: the middle class. Sounds simple enough, but we appear confused about the whys and wherefores around all things class. We need to let go of our long-held conceptions and come to terms with what social structures and categories might be relevant for today. Like much to do with the middle, class is subjective and influenced by super powerful social forces. The facts, our individual thoughts and feelings, and how others relate to it all combine into an ever-changing view of the class system and how we all fit within it. It is time to acknowledge its power, and to rethink and redefine class, and to think again about the middle class in particular. That way we will be better prepared and able to be in it, or around it, and use class dynamics to help us be us, and to use them as a force for good. This chapter takes a look at all of this and its relation to our own place, and asks we use this as a force for good.

2. Age

All of us have an age, and throughout our lives we grow older every year. There are several phases in our lifetimes as our body clocks ceaselessly tick away. These stages have been shifting over recent years, and we all have individual relationships with the concepts they stimulate. Naturally, I am interested in the middle age and I have aimed to put that into a contemporary context for all of us.

In simple terms, the middle age is the period in the centre of our lifetimes. However, it is difficult to agree when this is, what it means, and what to do about it. I am not alone in thinking the constructs of middle age are outdated, they no longer seem to reflect the way in which we live, work, and behave in the twenty-first century. The trouble is, we don't know when the middle age is supposed to start or finish, and we don't all agree on what it looks and feels like. We also struggle to work out what to do when we are approaching it, when we are in it, or when we have emerged on the other side. Too many of us are unprepared for it, or falling over at this point, which is terrible because we will miss the chance to revel in all its joys. I think we would all benefit if we better embraced our middle age, and I aim to show how we can. This chapter seeks to recontextualise middle age, reposition it, and to help positive attitudes and decisions so we can have the best experiences in the run up, when we are in it, and afterwards for that matter.

3. *Child*

Next, I look at the middle child who are those born or brought in, or who find themselves blended into a family and become the child in-between younger and older siblings.

There is lots learned in our childhoods, particularly our relationships, positions, and status – and we carry all that with us throughout our lifetimes. Middle children will very likely be aware of their position and may have learned a lot by being a middle child. Most certainly they will have experienced what it is like to not be the oldest or the youngest, and may know exactly how they feel in the middle – that maelstrom of familial observation, positioning, dynamics, and negotiation. As a result, middle children have a uniqueness. Their parents have possibly given them more freedoms than first borns. Their older sibling(s) may have been great mentors or at least demonstrated the do's and don'ts of childhood. They may have honed caring skills as they have nurtured their younger brothers or sisters. As such, middle children have potential to offer society, their families, and the world of work their invaluable and unique insights. They may have developed essential and exceptional skills for life, work, and in their own friendships and relationships. This chapter asks one simple thing, that we look at the middle child in terms of benefit not deficit, and to use that to support middle children to find and enjoy their rightful place.

4. *Work*

A big part of life for many of us is work. Work is a potential riot of conflicting and conspiring factors all relating to the middle. This is an environment, like our relationships that is influenced by our early experiences, and the intersections of our middles like family order, class, and age.

Lurking somewhere in the centre of many organisational structures is middle management. This isn't a term naturally associated with the hurly-burly of industry, creative innovation, or of career highs. Middle managers aren't the top leaders, yet they are above the workforce in the structure below them. They can occupy that uncertain place between the cut-and-thrust of decision-making and the dynamism of delivery. Often considered to be something that gets in the way, middle management is accused of slowing things down or overburdening everyone else. It is a reality of work, and something not properly considered. I wonder, has a schools careers adviser ever recommended to a student they would be a perfect fit for middle management? I guess not. This is such a shame. We need to find how essential the middle tier is in business functionality and performance. I think it would be wonderful if middle management basked in the sunlight it deserves. It really ought to be something to aim for, be much better valued, and be more usefully deployed. This chapter sets out the importance of giving the middle at work the attention and investment it needs, so organisations and individuals can get the best out of it.

5. Ground

In the final chapter, we look at the issue of viewpoints and explore the middle ground or place, something interesting in itself, and highly relevant to all other middles. Our views and opinions, politics and choices, are all informed by our place in society, our perspectives gained through age and experience, our position in the family, and our role and status if we work.

My view is that it's perfectly okay, if not desirable, to be in a middle place or be happy in the middle ground wherever that may be. It seems completely reasonable and sensible to me. And to be sensible need not be boring. It can be a confident, well-informed, open and accessible space for us all to dwell. In it, we can achieve the peace and quiet we could all be aiming for.

The middle truly is a place and a force for reconciliation and harmony, and it can be a space full of friendship and community. We can all learn to live and love the middle. This is my manifesto. This chapter includes all of that and aims to show how politics and place offer the joy and rewards from being reasonable in the middle.

So, there we have it, five distinct middles, with various overlaps and meeting points along the way. It's time we look again at what we are told, before we reconsider what we and others think, so we can inform a better way forward.

It seems many of us are in trouble with our conceptualisation of and relationship with the middle – all middles. We all need to think much more carefully, that means us considerately filtering out much of the nonsense that has come to surround middles, and to reinvent them. Let's look at two positive ideas.

Be More Robin.

In A. A. Milne's poem, Halfway Down, the middle (halfway) point is not at the bottom, and it is not at the top. It isn't anywhere, but somewhere else. It may be a compromise, an indeterminate state, the middle of nowhere perhaps. The poem was made more famous by the rendition of the Harold Fraser-Simson song (Halfway Down the Stairs) sung by Robin the Frog (Kermit's nephew on The Muppet Show in the 1970s – series one, episode 10 if you're curious). He sang *"It isn't really anywhere! It's somewhere else instead!"* I giggled lots when I saw it for the first time, I was probably eight-years-old. The record made it to number seven in the UK pop charts and they say it was sung at Jim Henson's funeral.

Robin seemed safe and quietly content halfway down. In contrast to those common feelings of disquiet. If you are content in the middle, I am pleased for you, and you should be proud of yourself. You have somehow found a way through the labyrinth of negativity and resiliently carved out a lovely spot for yourself. I want us all to pinpoint, share, and learn from that, for us to be more Robin, and occupy the place(s) we all want to be, like Robin's middle step of contentment.

Milne's poem is a charming reflection on a still moment of contemplation. It's about that special moment or location on the stairs, symbolising a place that is neither here nor there. This place serves as a metaphor for an in-between state, where we can stop and ponder life's various paths and possibilities. Always a good idea in my view. The stair represents a middle ground, a place away from value-laden destinations. Offering a place of rest, reflection, and imagination. Milne finds this spot to be unique and significant, as it allows for a break from the journey of life, offering a space to entertain *"all sorts of funny thoughts"*.

In essence, it captures the heart of those moments in life when we find ourselves in transition, neither fully engaged in activity nor completely at rest, but in a thoughtful space in between. It's a celebration of the small, often overlooked moments that offer peace and a welcome chance to dream. That sounds great to me.

Be more Bernie

I loved, loved, loved it when Gaylord Focker's parents, sex therapist Roz and retiree Bernie (adeptly played by Barbra Streisand and Dustin Hoffman), revealed their 'wall of Gaylord' displaying all of his middling achievements (Meet the Fockers, 2004). There were no gold medals, no first prizes. Quite the opposite actually. Male nurse Gaylord, hilariously played by Ben Stiller, was viscerally embarrassed, awkward, and confused by his parents' unquestioning and unwavering pride in him and his apparent lack of impressive achievements. Heartbreaking, as he was failing in his attempts to impress Jack, his rigid and high-performing potential father-in-law (Robert de Niro, no less), who remarked he *"didn't know they made ninth place ribbons"*. The subtext being his obvious disapproval that his son-in-law was a nurse, not a doctor or a surgeon. His loss I say. Jack no doubt always came in first place or in the top three. He will have passed all his exams. That's privilege that is. For the rest of us, finishing unplaced in the indiscernible podium-free middle, is the reality. Bernie tells us it *"isn't about winning or losing, it is about passion. We just wanted him to love what he is doing."* Well said that father. Maybe we should all be more Bernie. He was a true champion.

Living a real life.

It's not all good though, there are troubles ahead. In the 1998 movie, The Truman Show, Jim Carey played Truman Burbank who was controlled by a god-like, ruthlessly manipulative, television producer. Unbeknown to Truman, the entirety of his 30-year long life had been a scripted reality, broadcast 24 hours a day, seven days a week on TV. A show on an epic scale, it had become a global phenomenon. The whole of the world watched his every moment, and the TV company and its advertisers were raking in the dollars. The only person unaware of this was Truman himself, who as an orphan, had been incarcerated on a gigantic island stage set, surrounded by a cast of hundreds. His parents, his girlfriend, his friends, all actors cast in their roles. At first, to the viewer, it all seemed a peachy 1950s utopian dream. Then Truman's curiosity was raised, he started to think his world wasn't as real as he had previously thought. Then the whole story, Truman's self, and the TV producers' careers all spectacularly unravelled. Truman came to realise his whole reality was faked. A prison of sorts. His and all our dreams became a living nightmare as we all realised his life was at a pivotal moment and what happened next was going to be up to him and no one else. He was in his middle age, and the familiar tale of a so-called midlife crisis unfurled before our very eyes. So many of us can be like Truman and enjoy our constructed lives, thanks to society and our families, up to the point we look at it differently (whatever and whenever that is prompted by). And in giving such scrutiny to our lives we can start to question everything. This can be a difficult process, and it needn't be like that, instead it has the power to be transformational and positive.

Know that crises aren't inevitable.

Like Truman, some of us experience what is traditionally, and inadequately, labelled a so-called 'mid-life crisis'. It is too easy for our once robust and youthful defences to be chipped away over the years, and this dissolves our resilience to the point of fragility or even collapse. These episodes, of feeling unhappy, aren't exclusively experienced by people of a 'certain age' or of a particular place. Crises are said to be promoted by the recognition of a deep sense of apparent and relative directionless under-achievement or unrealised dreams. Given what we know about the middle already, it is clear the conditions for this to happen do exist. Career crises can also occur, when you feel unsure about what you are doing, and why, and cannot see the route map out of what may feel like a workplace trap.

How dare we allow society or work to treat us this way? We should instead be designing a world of awakening and opportunity in the middle. We need to be investing in these important years to build or maintain our resilience, so we prevent this from happening at all. That means we need to be ready by putting in some ground work.

The middle cannot continue to be something for mere amusement nor extreme ridicule. It should become a goal. For anyone to feel like a life failure is just morally wrong, and emotionally unfair. Because to realise a happy place somewhere in the middle can be a truly wonderful thing. It is real. We need to take on Robin and Bernie's approaches and let go of Gaylord's awkward feelings of humiliation and underachievement, and wear those ninth placed ribbons with pride.

Be conspicuous by your presence.

Carl Jung said normal *"is the perfect aspiration of the unsuccessful"*. That's a huge disappointment. It is rude actually. There are mixed messages here of course. To be normal or average isn't a failure or lack of success. It is, as I say, realism. Not a lack of aspiration, but a tangible, achievable, and rewarding position. That's where me and Carl (we're on first name terms, you know) differ. And it's where I agreed with Elton John, played by Taron Egerton, who said in the emotionally intelligent biopic 'Rocketman' (2019) *"Maybe I should have tried to be more ordinary"*, he imagined being inconspicuous, when reflecting on how difficult his life had become in an interminable spotlight. Despite its advantages and opportunities, it seemed as if he was saying it was easier not to be famous and successful. It probably is. The reality is the easiest option is to 'fit in', if you can find where you fit in.

I have a dislike for the phrase normal, that's not unusual, many share that view. The whole concept of normal has always been steeped, rather unhelpfully, in ethnocentricity, heterocentricity, and gendercentricity. I know some of those are made up words, but you get my point. Normal, in western culture, and in my lived experience has been white, British, straight, and male. Not necessarily a bad thing, but the global majority doesn't fit that mould. Fellas, I must say the patriarchal society has let everyone else down over the years.

Rather encouragingly, new norms are now emerging that are breaking down many of the barriers and judgements upon which all our normality has been built upon. Whilst there's some way to go, TV and popular culture, the workplace, and society is much more diverse and inclusive these days. Light years from what it was like as recently as my childhood. When it comes to the normality of the middle, we need to continue to draw new lines in the sand. Trouble is for some, this can feel threatening to their held notions of normal, and that can breed terrible pre-extinction burst behaviours, examples of which are in the middle ground chapter.

Be better earlier.

Many of the problems are imprinted upon us when we are young, in our early years, and our perspective becomes indelibly formed. I know this because I have been a child, I have grown and developed, I have processed my thoughts and feelings, and I have received psychotherapy. I have also spent all my career working in the early education and childcare field, doing my bit to help children and young people to have access to high quality and impactful children's services. I am also a qualified psychotherapist. Therefore, I have worked to ensure children, before they start school, during their school years, and after, have the best formative experiences possible. And that they are safeguarded and protected from harm.

Childhood, especially the earliest years, is such an important time. Our brains develop so profoundly – especially in our first two years, we literally have the opportunity to positively wire children's brains in early childhood. In their early years, children can forge strong attachments with all their care givers. Their experiences develop the blueprint for cognitive functioning, their relationships, future lives, potential, psychology, and psychopathy. I have come to think we need to do things differently for our children. These interventions and investments should be formative, social, cultural, educational, and inspirational, and embedded with the benefits of the middle.

I have also worked with adult clients, who, for whatever reason needed to revisit those patterns and effects set in the foundation of their early life experiences and throughout their resultant adult lives. Seeing how their psychopathy has been informed by what they have experienced and learned as children helps a great deal, so they can reach a point of feeling good enough.

Take four steps.

Making sense of the middle, I have come to realise, is best achieved by using a four-step approach: 1) take an objective look at the facts; 2) consider our own attitudes and feelings; 3) then explore the relational factors (i.e. what others think); then 4) decide what action to take next. I shall use this structure in various ways throughout this book.

There are many ways in which we can undertake this thinking, and to make alternative lifestyle choices so we can achieve peaceful and accepting states of mind. I would like those who have struggled with middle concepts and/or transitions to adopt a more contented position. I think it could be a liberating force for all those middle children, middle class, middle aged, middle managers, middle thinkers, living or working out there.

Achieve peace with the middle, in all its variants, and happiness could be yours for the taking. Finding joy in the middle is a state of mind that values the important things in life and work. We can counter the historical and societal conspiracy and rewrite the narrative. That's what I believe, and I want you to believe it too. I hope to convince you, if I haven't already.

It is time to enjoy ourselves and celebrate. Nothing, especially existential pondering and denial, should be allowed to get in the way of this mission. But to achieve that, we need to reboot our thinking and that of others around us. We can shed the manacles of all this conspiracy. We must invest positive energy in redefining the middle and repurposing it. And construct our own futures.

The middle is the truth, and I want to tell it. I think we can all be happier in the middle. In all middles. Wherever your middle-point is, it is vital to be happy when you are there.

Before you start the first of the five main chapters, pause for a moment, garb a pencil (you'll need one later) and consider your gut feelings or instincts about all things middle. Make a note of them, and at the end of each of the five main chapters, take another look.

How many of these are you?
(Tick all that apply)

- Born a middle child
- Became a middle child
- Identify as middle class
- Don't want to be considered middle class
- A long way off being middle aged
- Approaching middle age
- In middle age
- Been through middle age
- Feeling old
- Worked/working in middle management
- Aiming to work in middle management
- Hold reasonable and fair public or private political views
- Occupy the middle ground at home
- Take the middle ground with friends

And how do you feel about the middle?
(Tick all that apply)

- Generally feel good about being in the middle
- Love being in the middle
- Aim for it
- Embarrassed by it
- Confused about what it is
- Actively avoiding it
- In denial about it
- Generally unhappy about the middle
- Hate being in the middle
- Not really thought about it much
- Don't want to think about it
- Thinking twice about reading this book
- Ready to move to chapter two

—————o—————

The middle class

"The distinctions separating the social classes are false; in the last analysis they rest on force."

———○———

**Albert Einstien,
theoretical physicist**

Einstein suggested the divisions between different social classes are not based on inherent or natural differences, possibly building on the thoughts of Marx there. Instead, these distinctions are maintained through the use of power and coercion. Essentially, Einstein was critiquing the societal structure that upholds class differences, implying such divisions were artificially constructed and perpetuated by those in power to maintain their status and control over others. Just like how history has been constructed to suit the convenience of the few. His statement reflected his views on social justice and his advocacy for a more equitable society.

That connects with what I think. Class systems remain and are reinforced by those in power, and those contained within them. Where power exists, and Einstein says it does, then we all have a responsibility to use it wisely and for the greater good. If you are in the middle of the system, you can be squeezed by its active forces from all sides. You may disagree and might be thinking that class, particularly the middle class, is simply not a relevant issue anymore. You may have disagreed with former British Prime Minister Tony Blair when he said in 1999 that *"the class war is over"*, as part of his vision of creating a new middle class of millions of people who may have traditionally seen themselves as working class. You may consider it futile, just not current, or something not worth contemplating these days. You may be wondering why this is included in the book at all. It would be such a missed opportunity if you skipped this chapter and went straight to the next (the middle age). I urge you to be patient, as middle age will come soon enough (if it hasn't already).

Some have declared class is over.

Class, some have asserted, is an anachronism. It finished in 1914, according to the English novelist D.H. Lawrence: *"nothing remains but a vast proletariat, including kings, aristocrats, squires, millionaires and working people, men and women alike. And then a few individuals who have not been proletarianised"*. Maybe this was just sarcasm. If we are to believe D.H., we are all the proletariat. We are all in the blue-collar working class. Even all those 'nobs' and 'toffs' that he listed. Over one hundred years on, I am sceptical.

Presumably his supposition was influenced by the end of the Victorian era, or the effects of the beginning of the First World War (1914-18). And that collective experience of distress and devastation of its effects, and doubtless a dramatic social levelling, as millions of people of all classes shared that truly awful and traumatic experience. War certainly breaks barriers. Maybe there was a uniting feeling of all being in it together, as the tragedy of war touched all classes indiscriminately.

But, I think class is still important.

You'd be forgiven for thinking class extraneous, given Lawrence et al have declared the very idea to be extinct or fluid to the point of irrelevant dilution. Perhaps your liberal or socialist leanings cause you to think you overlook class in everyday life. Possibly you consider class to be a tangible indicator and measure of inequality and disadvantage. Maybe your privilege and position hasn't prompted you to give it much thought. You may think the erosion of class is to blame for the deterioration of certain standards or manners in society. You might think it not a modern consideration at all. I mustn't put words into your mouth.

But if you are cynical and have suspicions, I aim to prove there are alternative views. This chapter isn't about encouraging you to be middle class, or to contain you with the definition of other classes. Instead, it is a contemplation of the middle in society's structures. This is important to me because class is powerful, and its powers aren't always deployed with best intent or positive consequences. I want you to think about class, reconcile your relationship with it, and think how you can use it as a force for good. If you are feeling uneasy about it, angry, ashamed, or uncomfortable, I would hope this chapter will help you to find some peace with it.

Class is very much at the root of today's social attitude, political ideology, social immobility, discriminatory legislation, inequality, and extreme harm. I will show that class can be a matter of life and death. That might surprise you, on first thoughts, but it really is an important matter for the middle.

Personally, I don't sign up to the idea we are all socially mobile to the extent the class system is archaic. You may, like me, be fascinated by the dynamics of class in our society. You may have noticed its visible and invisible currents, powers, and effects, and how these stretch across all of our private, public, and professional lives. You, like me, may have been personally affected by class issues – either in good or unfavourable ways.

Those who have broken ceilings might also disagree. Well done them I say – for breaking their own barriers and thresholds. They are the lucky ones – they are the Jacks. It reminds me of John Prescott, the left-wing union activist who became the deputy Prime Minister, when in 1997 he said *"we are all middle class now"*. The risk in this is that sometimes those that have 'made good' can develop short-term memories and become distant from the realities of the lived experiences of those that have not. That makes them think class is defunct or more elastic than it might really be.

Non-maleficence.

If you're of the view the class system doesn't exist, that you are perhaps one of those people in a privileged position where it has done you no harm. That is a fortunate position indeed. It has not got in your way. You either benefitted from it, or you simply have just not noticed how it works. The worry is you may be blithely unaware of how you are part of the class dynamic; I wonder what harm you may be causing as a result? Lawrence was the working-class son of a miner and factory worker. Perhaps the trappings of his own literary success had convinced him of social mobility for all and the end of the class system. I find that to be a common trait.

Many simply haven't observed or appreciated when class has harmed or impeded others around them. That's what privilege is. Maybe they are spending all their time with people with the same class characteristics. And this missed opportunity, this limited experience, is blinkering their view. It is stopping them from playing their part to break the constructed boundaries that class has created. What we do now is what matters. Take the lessons in this book. If you were to choose to approach it differently, you could be part of a new class and social revolution (with a small r), because with privilege comes Responsibility (with a big R).

Let's talk about class baby. Let's talk about you and me.

I believe class serves to satisfy the basic human need to identify and connect with our order, position, and social tribe. There is a tension here and throughout the book about social constructs and human instinct, as they have a symbiotic relationship satisfying and creating each other. Several categories of class still remain, and they are influential forces across all our personal and professional experiences and existences. These categories of class have been variously described for centuries, mostly based on inherited, material, and behavioural concepts. In polite society, it seems a bit rude to talk about class, it can rub against our instincts to avoid judging or labelling others. We need to put all that timidity aside for a moment (for this chapter at least) and take a good long look at class, and the middle class, within a modern context.

Lots of people are in the middle. The Pew Research Center (also simply known as Pew) is a nonpartisan US think tank based in Washington DC, in a 2015 survey, they found just 10 percent of Americans said they considered themselves lower-class and only 1 percent thought they were upper-class. The rest, you guessed it, considered themselves to be some sort of middle class, that was a staggering 89% or 295 million people. The truth is that far from the American Dream, being in the middle can be a global nightmare of unhappiness, dissatisfaction, and confusion if not properly and consciously considered. In the UK, a huge 60% of UK adults (c.30 million) are now classed as ABC1, which means they are in one of the three higher social and economic groups, consisting of people who have more education and better-paid jobs than those in other groups. You may not think self-identification is a reliable measure, and you would be right, class is subjective, and profoundly affected by social change – something the book explores in more detail.

When taking a closer look, I found the 2013 BBC Great British Class Survey identified and described a model of no less than seven classes:

1. **Precariat**
2. **Emergent service workers**
3. **Traditional working class**
4. **Working class**
5. **Technical middle class**
6. **Established middle class**
7. **Elite**

At first that seemed like a surprisingly long list. Surely it could be and should be smaller than that? Even with so many categories, elite seemed to me to be too broad alongside the others. The elite surely included those with inherent and inherited power, privilege, deep-pockets, and political sway. I think therefore that it needed to be subdivided to include royalty, the aristocracy, and the ruling or political classes (but even in political classes there are political parties and characteristics that are based on issues of class and privilege). Of course, not all societies have royalty or the aristocracy in their traditional sense, and sometimes where they don't exist, they are replicated; think Hollywood royalty.

There seemed a gaping chasm between the elite and the next category which was the first middle – 'established'. I was intrigued to see a separation of the middle into 'established' and 'technical' class. The technical middle class was new to me, as was described as having high economic capital but less culturally and socially engaged than the others in the established (inter-generational or inherited) middle classes. This suggested that to be 'connected' was an important feature of one's social (middle class) status, and that doing well economically and collecting the trappings of the supposed middle class wasn't quite enough to grant full middle class status. Funny, given that is probably me and my class definition.

I was familiar with the thought of upper middle class, middle class, and lower middle class. Maybe this two-way split was a device to define the upper echelons of the middle and a way to appease 'old money middles' who can become a little sniffy if they feel their brand being diluted by the vulgarities of 'new money'.

A three-way split of the working class was interesting too, those being working, traditional working, and emergent. For me this set out a difference between working class professions and jobs and indicated a possible blurring of the boundary with the technical middle – I couldn't see how this could be a hard separation. I wondered how someone became technical middle or working class. In all areas where there are categories, there are of course examples that sit on the fence, or have feet in both camps.

Emergent service workers, let me explain, were a new, young, urban group of people. They are relatively poor but have high social and cultural capital, and potential. A reflection perhaps of the prominence of the service industry in modern day employment, and the stealth like extension of working lives.

Overall, these seven categories seemed too little in some areas, and too much in others. What happened here was the researchers had designed a way to measure class. They had aimed to move beyond the notion of defining class by the job a person had. That seemed sensible enough given how diverse roles have flourished in areas such as technology and services in recent years. Instead, they defined categories of held capital in three areas: economic, cultural, and social. They asked about income, home and savings values, activities and behaviours, and the number and status of people they knew. A huge 160,000 people completed the survey, which the authors asserted was one of the largest ever studies of class in Britain. Who's not to argue?

In addition to detailing seven categories of class, researchers acknowledged the very rich and the very poor still existed in society. Something I would venture has only become even more extreme in the years since. I wondered if and how things have changed, and whether we were just more aware of the chasm between society's advantaged and disadvantaged. Naturally, in my fascination of what exists in the middle, I wanted to think more about what that space was between the two.

There were other key observations I was pleased to see, even from a survey well over 10 years old. They found the traditional working class was changing, indeed it was thought to be getting smaller, as a result of the growing (actual or perceived) affluence of some, and the emergent legions of service workers. People's cultural engagement and identities are ever more complex, with the technical middle and working classes less engaged than traditional middles.

Mainly, I have found we talk about four different classes: upper class, middle class, working class, and lower class. I favour this simpler approach, with some caveats (actually a few). Of course, my focus is unsurprisingly on the middle - but I will put that into context of all of these.

In the iconic 1966 BBC Frost Show class sketch, upper class John Cleese, wearing his bowler hat and pinstripe suit, admitted to looking down upon the other classes. Those being the trilby wearing, lounge suited middle class man played by Ronnie Barker, and the cloth-capped and mac coat wearing lower-class man Ronnie Corbett. Cleese, despite his lack of money, felt above both because of his *"innate breeding"*. I don't really know what this means – do you? I would guess he means his inherited nature, birth rights, and entitlement. Barker, said that although he had money himself, he looked up to the upper class. He appreciated he was *"vulgar"* – lacking in the sophistication or good taste defined by the upper classes. The only compensation of being in the middle classes for Barker was the opportunity to look down on Corbett, the lower class, poor, industrious and trustworthy working class man who *"knows his place"*.

Beatle, John Lennon was right when he sang Working Class Hero: *"as soon as you're born, they make you feel small"*. I don't think it was a coincidence that Corbett played the working class chap, who stood at 5ft 1" (155cm). Lennon's song served as a commentary on the difference between social classes, reflecting the process of the working-class being moulded into the middle classes, to become part of the societal 'machine'. It was a warning to those from working-class backgrounds to resist the pressure to conform to societal norms and was a challenge to think beyond one's place. The stuff of revolutionary thoughts.

All of that, I believe, needs to be put into a relevant position for today, some 60 years later. But first we need to consider all those different classes, starting with the lower class.

The lower class.

Nothing feels more discourteous in polite society than referring to the lower or under classes. Indeed, there was no representative of the lower class in the Frost Show sketch. The lower class don't work and have no wealth or property. They instead are at the 'bottom' of the social class hierarchy, with the lowest status, and worst formal educational achievements. As such, I guess they just weren't funny enough to be included in The Frost Show. They were tragic and not entertaining.

The lower class have the least money, most insecure housing, uncertain citizen status, and they live invisibly and far below the poverty

"As soon as you're born, they make you feel small."

———o———

John Lennon

line. They have been failed by their families and society, and experience the worst that life brings.

The lower classes have the greatest barriers in the way of their social mobility. Like women, their invisibility was evident in the Frost sketch, and their exclusion and their lack of voice and representation continues to this day. Some say things are getting worse. In these days of high immigration, asylum seeking, population migration, and unfit-for-purpose systems and processes, their numbers are booming.

The working class.

I have always vehemently identified myself as working class. Why? Well, I was born into a working class family; a working class farm labourer family stretching back more than 500 years. I have grown up and lived in working class areas, I have worked for a living. I speak with *"flat Northern vowels"* (according to feedback). Those are my facts.

Working class was always, for me, defined as people who needed to work to live – and still is. Corbett was not lower class (or lower working class for that matter), he was working class, described as hardworking and dependable. He was no doubt paid wages by the hour at the end of the week, and he paid rent. Seems simple enough, doesn't it? In the 1960s, working class jobs included manual labour, and roles below that of management, or business ownership. Those were for the middle classes or higher.

The lower working class experience a set of more precarious conditions. The term precariat, a blend of precarious and proletariat, was said to be coined by the economist Guy Standing. He combined the words to describe the reality of low-wage workers in our modern, global economy. The precariat refers to an emerging, multi-dimensional class of workers who face unstable employment conditions and increasing uncertainty. Standing's work highlighted the challenges faced by this group due to labour market flexibility, temporary jobs without benefits, and other strategies that reduce labour costs in the pursuit of global capitalism.

It seems I am not alone in identifying as working class. In the 2016 British Social Attitudes survey, 60% of respondents identified as such. But this may or may not be an accurate assessment. My suspicion is this self-identification is affected by the blurred boundaries of various lifestyle indicators and the workplace becoming much more diversified and service sector driven. Jobs are so different to how they were before. It simply isn't as easy as thinking about farmers, miners. and factory workers anymore. With a dissolving of traditional jobs, government funding changes, the growth of the service industry, and mercurial career paths, and to be the planners of their own work journeys. It is more common these days for people to set up their own businesses, and run them and grow them, or they can have fluid freelance careers – something that is also precarious (but in a middle class way). This is one of the roots of the problem of deciding where the working class ends, and the middle class starts these days. Because it used to be the middle classes, not the working classes, who were the ones that owned and managed businesses before.

The middle class.

The middle class, of course, is a group of people in the middle of social hierarchies. But the application of the term is ambiguous. Commonly described as a group of educated people, the middle classes are occupied in professional roles, such as management or business ownership, affording them a higher level of income paid through salaries (not wages). They have a certain social status, and they live in houses and pay mortgages (not rent).

Politically, there are divisions. Those on the right favour the traditional middle class traits, whilst left-leaning social theorists have an interest in those who have moved from their working class roots and assumed middle class characteristics (like Prescott) – through their technical and economic progression. The term can therefore be vague and inconsistently applied to suit these competing dogmas.

Ronnie Barker (Frost Show again) stood in the centre of the line-up (taller than Corbett and shorter than Cleese). He was between the upper and the working classes. He worked, professionally, and we are told he had plenty of money. He attracted criticism because he spent it in "tasteless" ways, those being the ways the upper class disapproved of (no doubt the ways the working class could only dream of). His consolation was he still had the working class to look down upon.

I confess, it has 'got my goat' when people have told me in accusatory tones that I was middle class. I didn't think I was – even though I tick most if not all those characteristics described a moment ago. It sparked an internal discussion and debate. Not that there is anything wrong with the middle class. I just didn't accept the commonly held view, and didn't see a match with my held definitions of it. Writing this book has helped me comes to terms with it for lots of reasons. During the past few years I have become middle aged, and I've learned a lot from reading, researching and talking to people about that and matters of class. I have noticed and contemplated my characteristics, how others relate to me, and the contents of my address book.

The upper class.

The upper class is a social class comprising people with the some of the highest social status. They are usually, but not always, the wealthiest. Their money, assets, and noble status have been passed from generation to generation. They often wield the greatest elected and unelected political power.

In that 2013 survey, the elite was how the upper class was described. They were the most privileged, with their economic capital setting them apart from everyone else. Cleese represented the upper class. His outfit was straight out of the City of London. A sharp pinstripe suit (bespoke and tailored), bowler hat, and an umbrella (presumably carried every day, if it was raining or not), and no doubt the socks were darned. All accoutrements of the stock exchange or the boardroom. The upper class then, didn't have to work, but they may choose to do so. And if they do, they are in charge. They hold various financial and political roles and responsibilities. Their existence is far from the lower classes' hand-to-mouth, the labour of the working classes, and beyond the aspiration and progression typified by the middle classes. Rather, there is a deep sense of taking care of the family wealth, stocks and shares, estates and assets, position and status, before the next generation takes on the mantle. A deep and innate feeling of responsibility. They don't always pay mortgages, they pay upkeep of the properties they are mere custodians of, they may draw a salary of company dividends, or they live off income from trust funds, whilst trying to survive the consequences of inheritance tax.

Royalty.

The upper class isn't the top of the pile though. The aristocracy and royalty have the very highest social status and wealth in the UK and in many other countries. This is the upper-upper class. If they do work, this is called 'service' or 'duty'. Like the upper classes they also have wealth and power. There is personal wealth of course there is, and some of this is the trappings of the role and their lineage, rather than individually held or controlled. The boundaries between the state and royal wealth can be blurred.

In transportation terms, whilst the working class might have a van, the middle class a company car, royalty will have a horse drawn state carriage or fleet of chauffeur driven limousines (not the ones used by bachelorette parties - they are most definitely working class).

There are different rules. A royal is thought thrifty if seen to be wearing the same outfit twice. What's different here is the sense of being born into a role where there is limited choice. Futures are predetermined – that's the class system at it again. Roles and functions are integrated into public and political life. Life is the job, the job is the life, all lived out in the public gaze. For some of them, they complain it feels like a trap from which they want to escape. One of them recently drew parallels with the Truman Show, mentioning no names, obviously.

The modern middle class.

These traditional categories and characteristics give us some reasonably reliable and simple clues to what today's middle class may be. That's how it seems to me anyway. Using these simple and traditional indicators, even without the benefit of an online questionnaire, a middle-class family has been easy to spot. If the father was in a professional role such as a doctor, and mother was at home (or also working in a professional role), and there were books, the family sat down together at dinner time and ate at lunchtime then they were almost certainly middle class.

Nowadays the careers, the mortgage, the household rituals are much less reliable. A result of changing workplaces, professions, a growth of home ownership in the working classes, university attendance, and social and behavioural fluidity.

So, it may be helpful to go back to basics. If we use the tried and tested approach of thinking about what the middle isn't, that might make things a little easier. Middle class isn't lower or working class, nor is it upper class or royalty. Again, the middle is in that space in-between. As Hilaire Belloc observed:

> *The people in between*
> *Looked underdone and harassed,*
> *And out of place and mean,*
> *And horribly embarrassed.*

That seems reasonable. Those in the middle do feel embarrassed or awkward about it, especially when children identify as a different class to their parents or other relatives – a situation commonly created by university education. There is also the shame of not being in the upper echelons, to have not quite made it, or to be not included. The inner turmoil of the guilt-ridden middle, without the solace of knowing one's place like those in the lower and working classes.

Nowadays, classifications are created using all sorts of hard and soft information. This is because, as free thinkers, we all start to develop ideas and thoughts about how we self-identify or judge others. We also notice how others recognise us or relate to us, and how they perceive us to be. There is inter-personal and intra-personal conflict there when we don't like what we hear.

There is more to being middle class than the bare bones of assets and wealth, like it used to be, there is muscle and cartilage to consider as well. As those traditional categories and definitions have been chipped away, class has become more about preference, culture, and politics. These have all become the indicators or measures to reach new classifications, for example, the working class work fewer hours than they did a century ago, and that, along with all the other benefits of modern living (health care, labour saving domestic machinery, transport etc.), means they have the time, and the inclination to pursue what were traditionally thought to be middle class pastimes (like travelling, or going to the theatre) instead.

The narcissism of small differences.

People have started to notice characteristics that, for them and for society, have built their own sense or self-identification of class. Now, I am not closed to these ideas, I know the facts have changed hugely even within my lifetime. Let me say more – and share some of my voyage of self-discovery.

I have been to university (the first, but not the last, in my family to do so). I have developed a professional career, owned and run my own business, and I own my own home. Some of my behaviours, pastimes, and tastes reveal so-called middle class traits as well – things like the theatre, travel, art, and dare I say it, dinner parties.

In the past, I have rejected any idea or accusation I was middle class. And I use the term 'accusation' deliberately. Because people appear to revel in what seems like a new-found hobby of the class-coding of those around them. It's part of how we, as social animals, try to work out how and where we fit in with others, where those around us fit, and how we manage to keep up with the Jones', the Patels, or the Farquharsons. We all need and want to know where and how we size up, no matter how small the differences.

Social class categories are too broad for some of us – even when there are seven of them. And their applications and interpretations are so fluid these days. This is why I have my own internal tussles with class, there doesn't seem to be a natural fit. Most of us want to be different, we want to be seen to occupy our own unique place(s) in our communities, families, and at work. We want to self-identify. Difference is a good thing, as long as it is respected and is used positively. The risk is that many of us want to live our lives on smaller self-identifying islands rather than harmoniously on a tolerant and diverse continent. That can be the stuff of division, disrespect, and conflict.

The narcissism of small differences was a theory, started by British anthropologist Ernest Crawley. It occurs when communities with adjacent territories and relationships are likely to engage in disputes and mutual ridicule caused by hypersensitivity to details of differentiation. Literally to create the very small differences that stimulate class difference, niggles, tensions, battles, and ultimately wars. The term was devised, and the thesis extended, by Sigmund Freud in his Introduction to Psychoanalysis in 1917. I love it, and I know I overuse it if I am completely honest. So many of us want to appear different and special, I see it all the time, and often it feels artificial and unnecessary. To engage in such behaviours reveals to me there is something lacking in their psychology. For what purpose do people crave such micro-notoriety I wonder?

The very rigidity of objective class definitions must be driving some people's desire to sub divide it. It may be promoting people's longing to be class fluid and to self-define. People may accept they are one class or the other, they might even be insistent or have deluded or contradictory ideas. They may want to be royal (they may be determined to marry into it) or enjoy the superficial reality of royalty without the shackles of its historical, solemn, and ceremonial duty. What appears to drive such desires, to me, is people wanting to create distance from others they feel the same as, and to safeguard their want to look up or down on others. They may want the world to see them as they want to be seen.

This very much sounds like aspiration to me. When the economy is doing well, the differences are more convivial. In recession, or depression, then anger can simmer – fuelled by all types of injustice, disadvantage, and poverty and can result in high levels of dissatisfaction, conflict, riots, or even worse. We saw that in the UK when in the early seventies there was a feeling that social class was becoming irrelevant. Fast forward to the recession and mass unemployment later in that decade and into the 1980s then society developed an opposite view. The working class were on strike. Thatcherism was on the rise. Life became more divisive again. Battles were held on the coalfields. Riots occurred in the inner cities. UK Prime Minister Margaret Thatcher said there was no such thing as society. I think she was encouraging us all to be more selfish, self-centred, wealth driven, uncaring, and unsocial beings by saying that. Which seemed to me to be characteristics of her policies and government activities.

In 2024, in the UK, societal shifts and the injustices felt by the lower working and working classes created the underlying conditions for social media fuelled riots and looting in the streets of very many disadvantaged and marginalised communities. In response the working and lower middle classes also took to the streets, in much larger numbers and stemmed the uprising. Class war on the streets, all about differences, with the potential (some said) to become a civil war.

These tensions are real and tragic, and they are current issues. People sadly die in these riots, battles, and wars. The scale of death in such social unrest can be extraordinarily huge across the world, as history has shown us.

'Othering' has tragic consequences.

Discrimination occurs when a target person or group is subjected to the effects of denigratory beliefs, feelings, or actions on account of their membership or attributed membership of a group. It targets any difference from the perpetrators' 'norm' or intent. Othering defines people as not fitting in with the norms of the dominant group.

The notions of class, and other social characteristics are constructs with many layers. They are based on the idea that what people look and sound like determines them, for now and forever. Things like background, nationality, accent, skin, eye, and hair colour; and size, shape and pattern of other bodily features.

In modern times, we are exposed to so many multiple factors that influence our perception of difference. As a society, we travel more than ever before, and migration is super-charged. Which means society enjoys rich difference economically, and in class, cultural, or racial terms. This may be blurring what was, as recently as one-hundred years ago, more clearly defined. It certainly is fuel to the fire of fear.

Hanging a monkey.

Prejudicial myths are the products of fear, lack of knowledge, or low awareness. Here is an example. During the Napoleonic wars, a bizarre and legendary event took place in Hartlepool in the Northeast of England. At the time, there was a fear of French invasion and much public concern about the possibility of French infiltrators and spies. During the war, a ship was wrecked off the coast. Among the wreckage, only one survivor was found, the ship's pet monkey. It was dressed in a military style uniform said to be for the purposes of entertaining the crew. The legend says the fishermen, unfamiliar with what a Frenchman looked or talked like, questioned the poor creature and held a trial on the beach. They concluded the monkey was a French spy and would be sentenced to death. The fishermen had no knowledge to suggest that their assumption was incorrect, and the monkey was not a Frenchman. The unfortunate creature was hung on the mast of a fishing boat.

There are in any nation, 'ethnic' groupings that determine difference. These ethnicities are also the basis on which racist hostility, and deprecating beliefs and behaviours are informed. Many of these traits we may apply to our understanding of class. They are the recipe of indicators that add up to our understanding and definition of the person or people stood before us. They feed that desire to look up, down, or differently on others.

Given these characterisations, people can be the subject of ethnically motivated racism through their 'different' religion, clothes, or the food they eat. It was the basis for discrimination and genocide during the Nazi Holocaust, when people were organised and murdered not only for their nationality, but for their faith, heritage, sexuality, lifestyle, or appearance (amongst other reasons). That is one example, there are many others.

The name's Blond, James Blond.

If ever you need and want a clear example of how societal attitudes have changed, then watch a 1960s/1970s James Bond movie. It is all there for you to see – sexism, misogyny, ableism, colonialism, the Cold War, and racism. Bond opens a lens to how attached people can be to their perceived norm, and their reluctance to embrace change. The iconic film role of Bond has deeply pervaded British and international culture for over 60 years. I rarely get into a taxi overseas without a driver asking if my surname is Bond. When London hosted the Olympics in 2012, the late Queen Elizabeth II and the then Bond, Daniel Craig, were stood shoulder-to-shoulder as part of the opening ceremony, actual and film royalty representing British culture. How modern.

When Craig announced his departure from his critically acclaimed role in 2021, there was a right royal bru-ha-ha around the idea of his replacement. The press speculated if they could be Black, or a female actor, or both. The arguments they presented for and against were pretty much standard fare. But don't let us forget the very outrage at the idea of Craig himself becoming Bond, a blond Bond, in 2005. Whole websites were dedicated to an anti-blond-Bond campaign. People could not imagine nor tolerate the idea of a fair-haired Bond. It seemed any deviation from the tall-dark-and-handsome stereotype of his predecessors was too much for too many. This was ridiculous then, all these years later it seems doubly ludicrous. Some of those websites are still there – check them out. At the time of writing, Craig's replacement had still not been announced. Perhaps the decision proved far too difficult.

It's okay to notice, on one condition.

When difference exists, everyone is capable of discrimination. There's nothing wrong or unnatural about noticing difference itself, everyone can detect difference between people, whether it is the way they look, sound, feel or even smell. It is not difficult and is not necessarily a bad thing. The positive essence of discrimination is about noticing the differences between one thing and another. It is the subconscious, unconscious, or instinctive second thoughts that can be more problematic if they are negative or skewed. They can become highly damaging, and this is what we need to reprogramme. A positive response to difference is to recognise it and respect it – and that is a good goal to have.

Discrimination and oppression is applied by using a wide range of methods and measures. It can be direct, indirect, and institutional – acts of commission or omission. An individual person may be the target of racism by being the focus of racist chants at a football match, being excluded from attending an event because it has been scheduled during a cultural festival, their views and opinions are not asked or listened to as there is a language barrier, or being required to follow a dress or uniform code that does not allow for religious or cultural difference.

I told you class was important.

These situations, and many more, demand our attention and action. If we don't act, in whatever small or large ways, we are complicit in extending its effects. Words are just one aspect, silence is another. Not speaking up in defence of someone is action. Symbolic actions are more about public relations it seems than systemic change holding people to account. Small gestures are just that. It takes more than a corporate rainbow lanyard to be a sexuality or gender inclusive organisation. It isn't enough to include women or gay people in your organisation, or allow them to be members, consumers or customers, if they are excluded from consultation, prevented from getting the top jobs, are required to pretend to curtail behaviours, or are ignored in decision-making.

The sad thing is that so often people simply look the other way. Inaction is action. *"A person may cause evil to others not only by his actions but his inaction, and in either case he is justly accountable to them for the injury,"* said English philosopher and founder liberalist John Stuart Mill in On Liberty (1859). *"Throughout history, it has been the inaction of those who could have acted; the indifference of those who should have known better; the silence of the voice of justice when it mattered most; that has made it possible for evil to triumph,"* said Haile Selassie, former Emperor of Ethiopia.

Take some revealing tests.

You may already have a clear idea or view about where you fit. You may be confused, or uncertain. My advice is don't spend too much of your valuable time defining your class status, leave that to other people who haven't anything better to do. But do read on as the following 'tests' will either help or serve to further confuse you even more. I rather enjoy them I must admit.

The following considerations have been developed to suggest a whole range of signs and indicators that you might find useful when pondering your classness, and that of those around you. They might even stir up some emotional and social responses for you. That would be interesting.

As we have learned, social classifications traditionally grouped similar levels of wealth, influence, and status. Sociologists have typically used three methods to determine social class, based on facts, self-view, and the thoughts of others:

- An objective method reviews measures and analyses 'hard' facts. These are the things that I hold onto,79 to define my own sense of my class, like working and wealth.
- A subjective method asks what we think of ourselves. These are the signs that we ponder and recognise, as they occur in the

thoughts of others and across society, and we use them to reconcile and evaluate thinking and our relationship with class.

- A reputational method asks what people think of others. This is the opportunity we gain when talking to others and listening to their thoughts and ideas. I like to think of it in relational terms – how do people relate, observe and perceive you? It is the impressions you make on others. It's what and how you make them think and feel. How they interpret you, your behaviours, the signs, and indicators around you. These are somewhat out of your control.

The problem with the objective model is the hard facts can be too rigid and don't always match contemporary behaviours and lifestyles. Definitions of class are deep-rooted and mostly historical. The nature of modern society is it is fast moving and there is much change and nuances, characteristics are under sustained attrition, for example, attending university (a traditional class indicator) has been revolutionised in recent decades.

The trouble with the subjective and reputational methods is they aren't solid enough for me. They are too subjective and open to far too much personal interpretation open to the influences of social change, and informed by people's personal experiences, politics, and perspectives.

So what considerations are there? How can we reach reason?

- The university test.
Elites may have attended university, but they didn't always have to do that to gain further privilege. It was the established middle class people who typically did. However, all this has shifted even in my relatively short lifetime. University attendance can no longer be a reliable measure of established middle-class-ness. Fewer young people went to university in the twentieth century, and they studied classic subjects like languages, history or medicine or so it seemed to me. But in the twenty-first, so many more young people attended university and studied a multitude of new subjects. Polytechnics were converted into universities, which

was a deliberate, organised and politically motivated erasing of the class divide in Higher Education. A good move I reckon. Certainly, a nimble one. Going to university had quickly become an expectation for a new generation, who aspired to go, and subjects became much more diverse in response to the changing world of employment – and fuelled a boom of the technical middle classes.

Given the rising debt of students, the ballooning fees, and the apparent disconnect between the subject studied and the career that follows, things are changing. Government, young people, and their parents have been looking at other ways to enter employment and reject such investment and debt in favour of earlier income generation. I am pleased to see the pendulum swinging in the other direction to provide some balance. I am thinking about things like apprenticeships, vocational training, lifelong learning, more transference in terms of qualification application, or even dare I say it, work.

The concept of middle class has been under the influence of this student proliferation. There has been an enormous growth that anyone living in a university town (or two university town) will confirm. However, there are still disproportionately low numbers of working class students in universities, especially in Oxbridge or Russell Group, despite their positive initiatives.

Surely, going to university cannot alone cause someone to become middle class. Not now university is so different to what it was. I guess it also has something to do with what you do with your degree. A degree in philosophy, politics and economics can be a passport to join the ruling elite – a fast track to becoming an MP nowadays (which I think is a shame without practical policy and delivery experience). It is also more about which university and what subject you studied. I am very much of the view that too often students were being coaxed into science and maths under the mistaken view such subjects are more worthy to economic society. That is misguided, speaking as an design graduate, design skills are essential work skills and I use them every day in all contexts.

Non university options do prompt other questions. I mean, can you be a middle-class apprentice? I think so. Or is this the exclusive territory of the working class, let's face it middle class apprentices are known as interns. There is a financial difference here, apprentices are paid, and interns need to have their own means so they can work for free – a contract surely that only the privileged can afford to sign.

- The job test.
One's job cannot be a reliable indicator anymore. Once there were recognisable careers and professions. If you have a first-class degree in philosophy from Cambridge University, and you are working as a barista – what class does that make you? What if you were the owner of the café? What about your long-term plans? It is all so complicated. The job of the school careers' adviser was so much simpler then. I remember my choices being pretty limited to standard upper working or lower middle-class professions. I wasn't offered working class manual jobs (coal miner, farmer, builder), not a close match to my aptitude or physicality. There was the idea that I would work in an office in some sort of semi-professional role. With the explosion of new roles and professions since, there are debates about what makes a profession 'a profession' and how they fit into society's class structures.

Add to that and we can have multiple careers and professions concurrently or consecutively. You can make up your own career portfolio these days. The expansion of our life expectancy and our improving health creates the opportunity to have two or three careers or more. Something compounded by the economic realities of modern life, including pensions being paid later in life. It is common for people to start in a brand-new direction after what was traditionally middle, retirement, or post-retirement age (including returning to work). It is all very exciting. But it is hellishly confusing when trying to agree class categories.

- The People Like Us (PLU) test.
Perhaps there are better clues are in our behaviours. We all have class codes and tribal habits, such as where we shop, what clothes are worn, the car or transport used, the food eaten, the music listened to, the things read, and pastimes and sports enjoyed. This is the difference between

Lidl and Waitrose, Primark and Joules, the bus and a Volvo, a butty and a flatbread, Stormzy and a symphony, Take a Break and Tatler, the footie and the rugby.

These codes are like magnets pulling together people of similar interests and backgrounds for mutual appreciation, reassurance, and benefit. They form groups of 'people like us' (PLU). A term I learned at an actual middle-class dinner party. PLUs recognise each other and huddle together at parties, weddings, the theatre or arts centre, on football terraces, at the rugby or golf club, at work, and of course in the boardroom.

In the club or boardroom culture you become a member if people like you decide you are a person like them. If the face or background fits, you are granted entry. Positive initiatives aside. *"Next time you're in a meeting, look around. If everyone there is like you, it's time to ask who's missing?"* said Dr Zoe Norris in Pulse Today. I've sat in enough awkward board meetings to know that if you're different, you aren't always welcome, valued, or listened to. Best advice is to try and tactfully fight your corner a few times, but you'll most likely have to leave. I did.

- The dinner party test.
When people ask you to their house to eat, it could be for a barbecue or to TV and chill. The middle classes have a predilection for supper or a dinner party, for the purpose of enjoying the shared qualities of their tribe. They can be serious networking and connection building (or breaking) occasions. At a dinner party, you will find yourself sat alongside carefully chosen and complementary PLUs, where one is asked: where one holidays; what one is reading (and you may notice that even though there are hundreds of thousands of books to choose from, they are all reading the same ones! – that's the power of tribes that is); and what concert, theatre or art exhibition has taken your fancy recently (again, mostly the same). Be prepared, you might also be required to talk about current affairs. A common (pardon the expression) topic I have found is the anguish about urban knife crime. Something, in some circles (not mine), discussed in between frequent trips to the loo

(sorry bathroom, or should it be toilet?), or terrace, to perhaps snort a line of coke or inhale a cheeky spliff. All seemingly oblivious to the social conditions that link one with the other. The middle class cocaine market directly funds and fuels the supply of drugs and suppliers' turf and gang warfare. It is one of the root causes of knife crime and the killing of our young people on the street.

And towards the end of the evening, when they ask you if you'd like coffee, it means it is time to leave. It's the *'fuckoffee'* moment. You've drunk too much of their wine, eaten the cheese, or they resent you pointing out the contradictions interwoven through their social politics. Talking of cheese…

-The cheese test.
Does the type of cheese you buy and eat define your class at all? What can be revealed by an organic aged brie, a pre-sliced processed cheese, or a bag of grated cheddar? And how do you eat it? Do you have a cheese course before dessert at your dinner party, or serve it in a butty for tea? And how do you cut it on the cheese board, do you dare cut off the nose? (in polite society cheese should be cut diagonally and not in parallel to the rind). If you didn't know, you do now, you are welcome.

My brother, during a trip to Waitrose, heard a woman loudly ask: *"Dahling. Do we have parmesan in both our houses?"* I'd say she was pretty much middle class, wouldn't you? Parmesan and two houses! Question is: established or technical middle? I would need more information to know for sure – maybe a recording of the accent, and perhaps a photograph or video clip. Nowadays, if I am in Waitrose with my 'darling', we often play what has become known as 'the parmesan game'. We shout it out and run. Such amusement. It could catch on. Go on, I dare you – play the parmesan game.

-The tea test.
In contrast, it is absolutely obvious to me that class and tea are inextrica-bly linked in English society. Our social and colonial history is steeped in tea. Less so coffee, that seems like an altogether modern consider-

ation. Coffee elitists are well practiced at casting their judgements on all aspects of coffee growing, making, serving, drinking etc. I must admit, coffee is a mystery to me, I have never liked it, and I have rarely drunk it. So, I will use tea as the next test. The tea test. How do you take your tea? People ask in polite society. This is a total minefield. Which variety, which brand, loose leaf, a bag – what type, a bag with a tag, a square bag, a pyramid bag, a round bag, plastic-free, organic or unbleached. All are significant sign givers. Do you make it in a teapot or a mug? Do you serve it in a mug or a teacup and saucer? Milk (and what type of milk) in first or later? I am not going to waste time on the intricacies of such matters. Safe to say, it is a big issue. Me? I take it green, made in a pot, loose leaf or a plastic-free unbleached bag with a tag, without milk. Make your own judgement.

-The delayed gratification test.

For all of us, there is a key question we might ask ourselves on a daily basis. Opt for pleasure now, or delay it? Delayed gratification has traditionally been an unambiguous indicator of class, and a difference between the working class and middle class man. Working class, no delay, middle class, delay.

The archetypal working class man would be in a rush on a Friday night, pockets filled with the week's wages, with a mission to spend it on ale or at the betting shop. A way to escape the harsh realities of life – until the regret filled conflict the next day with 'the wife' who needed the housekeeping or the rent. Both quickly coming to realise it will be another week of hiding behind the settee (not the sofa or the couch) when the rent man came to call again. The single working class man no doubt woke up equally remorseful, nursing the bruises and grazes from their anger fuelled brawls late into Friday night and Saturday morning. On the Saturday afternoon, they would retreat to the local football ground, in an attempt to blot out the consequences of their actions and to express more anger to boot.

The middle-class father will have no doubt invested some of the month's salary in the mortgage, ensured there was sufficient funds to run the household, and invested in pension contributions. Deferred satisfaction, and reward later, was king here.

These days, such traits are much more difficult to pinpoint. I think these concepts and behaviours have been under attack from the 'now' culture, the 'get famous quick' society. It's another blurring of the boundaries that used to separate out our classified behaviours.

In modern times, we subscribe to adages, things like 'you only live once' or 'live fast, die young'. Our lives are facilitated by cars, jet planes, television, the internet, credit cards, and now multiple and instant access TV streaming channels, and food delivery apps. They have all been step-changes in upping the pace of life the gratification it offers. You want something, you can have it now. You don't have to wait until 7.30pm to watch your favourite TV soap. A few clicks and it is playing live whenever and wherever you want. You don't have to wait until next week to watch the next episode, you can view it now whether you be on the bus, at your desk, or in bed. You don't have to go to a restaurant for food, it can come to you via bike courier within 20 minutes.

Our tolerance for delay, our ability to be patient, to put in effort to gain rewards are all qualities being systematically eroded. We don't have to wait for anything anymore. It is a high-tech industrial class and lifestyle revolution, the technological enabling of instant gratification has waged war on any sense of delay. This all goes a long way to diminishing any sense of purposefully and diligently working hard and with purpose to an identified goal. Want to lose weight? Then pop a magic pill, work with a personal trainer, drink weight-loss coffee, or turbot charge the results and have some of those GLP1s (skinny jabs). The trouble is all these things require significant effort. They are not simple quick-fixes. As a result, we have become greedier, bigger, and fatter - maybe because subconsciously we think harder times are ahead, or we are hedging our bets just in case. That makes me think of Freud.

The 'id', as Freud would put it, our basic selves – that part of the psyche driven by instincts and impulses, is driven by the 'pleasure principle' that seeks out pleasure, so we avoid the pain. And the pain we are trying to avoid is our cumulative sense of demise, personally, as a community, a culture, a nation, a global species. The more pain we feel or have felt, the more pleasure we seek out. Our recent unchecked pursuit of pleasure might be hiding a deep sense of pain in the global population derived from postwar trauma, or global warming fears.

We are given constant messages about the challenges experienced in the natural world; habitat destruction, species extinction, population migration (animal and human). That human population is so out of control we know that one day the good times will end and rationing and restrictions will be put in place.

The younger generation certainly holds on to a real sense of doom and gloom and pessimism about the future of our world. Which is a real concern to me. It is not good for our young people. They are so anxious their mental health difficulties and anxiety levels are through the roof. Those that have gone through university have left saddled with huge and artificial or fake debt. The concept of money damaged to such an extent it seems unreal, false, and contrived. Someone on the TV said the other day: *"why should I get a mortgage if North Korea is going to nuke us?"*.

So why wouldn't everyone reach out for pleasure? Pleasure is an escape from reality, it is a diversion, and escape. I read recently the fervent pursuit of the selfie was linked to young people's sense of impending death. That made me think of Jung. It doesn't really help any sense of long-term planning for one's middle or advanced age – does it? It's quite childlike. When we are young, we only operate through the pleasure principle and expect immediate fulfilment. Then it's all about basic needs, milk, food, and comfort. Later it is still about basic needs, it includes food and drink, with the addition of sex and procreation (for some, not all). But as time marches on, we learn that we must often wait for gratification. That hurts, especially if one gets to middle age and you still feel unsatisfied on whatever level. And the trouble with patience in middle age is there is a strong sense of time running out, and patience starts to feel like a waste of that finite time. That turbo-charges impatience, let me tell you.

There are reported benefits to delayed gratification. Many say it is one of the most effective attributes of successful people and their jobs, lives, physical, and mental health. But how long do we have to wait? What if there is a real sense of time ticking away, when panic can set in. Because we just aren't used to waiting anymore are we?

-The lottery test.

How can you escape working classness? A common strategy is to buy a lottery ticket. Some buy a scratch card or five, offering even less delayed gratification through its instant results played out in store, on the pavement outside, or in the shame-free sanctuary of home. Playing the lottery is mostly a working-class trait, as the lowest socioeconomic status groups have the highest rate of gambling. Some consider it a tax on poor people, and don't consider the give-back to good causes to be sufficient reparation. Winning the lottery is the working-class dream, offering emancipation from the drudgery of work, and opening the ability to buy stuff that posher people have like a big house, a driveway, or a hot tub. A lottery win offers a passport to freedom from the control of the ruling classes, to realise the dream of walking away from the world of work. An instant way to break the financial boundaries that surround class divides and social mobility and opportunity.

The more middle and upper class you are the more likely it is either a guilty, unspoken, or secret pleasure, or it is the object of sneering and judgement, or something you would never contemplate participating in (preferring those longer term/delayed payouts over and above the chance of the here and now).

-The presented credentials test.

Then there is the matter of how we present ourselves. Whether that be conscious or unconscious, deliberate or accidental. I find it funny how many in politics and public life have strived to promote their gritty, working class, person-made-good credentials. They seem to be attempting to deny their privilege, power, and their classness, to attract congratulations for their achievements, for which they feel they deserve all the credit. Or are they using all of this as camouflage like wolves in sheep's clothing?

I must resist that compulsion as much as I can – things like telling people I went to a comprehensive school, in the Midlands, having been born and raised in working class areas. It is tempting though, forgive me if I lapse on occasion. Presented credentials are how people weave into their narrative details about where they grew up, their family, the school and university they attended, their jobs, and their property or assets. Depressingly though, there's at least an equal number of our political leaders who appear tone-deaf to their privilege. They present a bumbling, upper class, and blundering persona. Let's face it, the only way is up if you adopt that approach. If you go in as perfect, then the only way is down. Like promoting family values, and then not following them. Being imperfect is the ultimate defence. Very clever indeed. Mentioning no names.

- The vocabulary test.
Language and the choices we make in using it are an interesting indicator as well. What do you call your headwear – a cap, a hat, a tiara, or a crown? How do you ask people to leave your house – do you tell them it's time to leave, offer them coffee, get the butler to show them out, or ring a bell? What do you call your mode of transport – foot, bike, bus, works van, train, car, helicopter, aeroplane, private jet, or carriage? Do you eat breakfast, brunch, lunch, dinner, tea, or supper? Our language choices offer all sorts of clues about someone's heritage, upbringing, social circle, education, and work.

What does all of this tell us?

All of this has told us that class is a matter of objectivity, subjectivity, and relatability. The objective facts can be tricky and unreliable these days. In searching for an understanding, I don't think the traditional and objective characteristics work anymore. What with the overlapping diversity of modern life, social advances, and a multitude of professional and semi-professional jobs, it's just too complicated.

As a result, we are left with grappling a multitude of various self-definitions and serious or often flippant self-complete tests (sorry if you think I fell into that trap). The consequences are wide ranging. For some they are advantageous and desirable – fashionable even, for others they are simply detrimental, demeaning, or dangerous.

I hope I have presented a compelling case that the class system remains. With that knowledge we have a responsibility to build a contemporary and deeper awareness of it. Class is an equalities issue that affects us all – it has potent power that can create the worst in human predispositions and behaviours. It is much more important we use those instincts for the benefit of ourselves and others. Class is a classic middle issue, as we seek to understand the 'pecking orders' and how we fit in it, and manage our innate desires for needing and wanting to fit in. We do this to fulfil the most basic needs for feeling safe, connected, and loved.

We can use class to bring us all together, not tear us apart. We can be more equal, open, more respectful, and informed about difference. To do that requires us to be stronger by letting go of our fears. I think it is important we use this thinking to ensure we aren't stuck in our ways, and in denial about who we are and the effects we have on others.

I started this project whilst rooted to the notion of my working classness for the reasons I have shared. That was my subjective choice, even when I was buying parmesan in Waitrose, chatting to the butcher, and attending university. For me, the middle classes were those firmly established through multi-generational factors. Then, along came that term – technical middle – describing those with their feet in the ground of the working classes and their heads in the skies of the middle. I woke up and smelled the cheese, and have finished this project identifying with that. I will continually test myself, holding myself to account, and using some of the tests in this chapter, and perhaps other challenges as they present themselves later in my life's journey. I accept that others around me will have their relational viewpoints. That is their right. It is your right.

———o———

The middle age

"Middle age is when your age starts to show around your middle."

———o———

**Bob Hope,
actor and entertainer**

It hurts when we laugh.

The middle age seems to be a highly amusing aspect of life – for some. It certainly is rich fodder for comedians and greetings card vendors. They poke fun at the losses associated with growing older, or the unwelcome gains in waistline inches. Beyond the smart one-liners, there is a plentiful supply of negativity in society, and a dearth of joy about the realities of middle age. Naturally, I am unhappy about that.

I mean, how often have you heard someone say *'oh that's so middle aged!'*? a stealth like attack delivered with critical intent, it's rarely a celebration, and never a compliment. So much so, I am starting to think the middle age should be a protected characteristic, and I'm a bit cross with myself that I used that 'funny' quote to start this chapter.

It's not anyone's fault, there are huge forces at work. The lack of proper literature on the matter doesn't help us to gain useful insight. Search any bookstore and, if you are lucky, you may find a small number of books. They attempt positivity with advice-a-plenty, and often a comedic or mocking thread. They laugh at the male 'midlife crisis', middle aged sex, the menopause (less so these days), and the manopause.

We can take the middle age more seriously than all of this. We need to stop laughing and take a good and proper look at the middle age once and for all. For me, there's much more positivity and opportunity to find in the middle age than people might at first realise. On reflection, this was probably my primary motivation for writing this book. To help us all find more joy in the middle age, as well as all other middles.

What is middle age anyway?

Earlier, I mused there was no such thing as middle age in the middle ages. Hopefully, the irony of that didn't escaped you there. Basically, there wasn't enough time or opportunity in the middle ages to reach what we would describe as the middle age these days. Then, as we learned, you were lucky if you made it through childhood and managed to reach 21 years old. The average life expectancy was around 45. Can you imagine what a super-challenging double whammy it would be, to be middle aged in the middle ages? We don't have to go that far back for evidence that many people died in their forties and fifties. Visit any Victorian cemetery and you will see the tombstones. It was probably a good thing to not live much longer than that. Life was hard, really hard, and the older you got, maybe the harder life became.

Fast forward a few decades or centuries and there is plenty of time for it. The common middle age really is a modern concept. Life is a whole lot easier and healthier and safer. Yes, there are problems, there always have been in, but relatively we are really very comfortable indeed. Don't believe those doom and gloom merchants that say otherwise. They do a great deal of damage to what could be our healthy sense of proportion and risk. And when things get out of proportion, things can become very emotionally tough.

Our mindset could be that middle age is a time for the best things of life, and a time that needs our careful and deliberate attention. US 'First Lady' Eleanor Roosevelt said: *"probably the happiest period in life most frequently is in middle age, when the eager passions of youth are cooled, and the infirmities of age not yet begun"*. A classic and useful example of looking back and looking forward. She also said at midday, the shadows cast in the morning (of youth) and evening (of old age) almost entirely disappear. Middle age then is a time to go out in the midday sun, along with the mad dogs and Englishmen. Wear sunscreen or a hat though – don't be silly.

Roosevelt was an enormously impressive source of wisdom and her many quotes provide useful guidance for us all. She was a contemporary of Swiss psychiatrist Carl Jung, who also had cause to compare the stages of life with different times of the day. He talked much about the morning and the afternoon. He said: *"The afternoon of life is just as full of meaning as the morning; only, its meaning and purpose are different"*. That's great advice. He was saying that both have equal value and neither sides of noon should think otherwise, whilst acknowledging the difference.

Jung called the elder years - those from c. 56 to c. 83 years the afternoon of life echoing Roosevelt's analogy of the passage of the sun through the sky from morning to night. Youth was morning, noon corresponded to the start of mid-life, and night was old age. Our sixth and seventh decades see some of our life energy wane, much as the sun's warmth declines as it sinks lower in the sky. Remember though, often the hottest part of the day is in late afternoon. Just as we need the full cycle of the sun to support life, so we are meant to live out the full cycle of human existence, and Jung recognised this. More than just living, he urged us to enjoy the afternoon of life and, to regard death as life's ultimate goal.

Whilst this has all been going on, there hasn't been enough of a focus on sharing the wisdom for thriving and surviving the middle age. If we can find the way to embrace these natural phases of aging and let go of unhelpful and outdated derision, then we can unlock more fulfilling lives. Given the lack of useful material in print, we need better advice – and fast.

Middle age is a new fact of life. And one that all our parents (and possibly grandparents) should tell us more about. If they did, then you are very lucky indeed. Parents, or anyone for that matter, could sit us down and share their valuable insights and experiences of the middle – let's start that big conversation. Instead, it really feels like an oversight or even a taboo. And how inconsiderate of grandparents to not stick around for those moments we realise we need their wisdom to navigate this next chapter of our lives.

Maybe they did talk about it, and you and I weren't listening. Any parent giving advice to a child or young person is a brave soul indeed. If any parent manages to get their offspring to pay attention, without the bribery of food, cash, or a lift/ride, then they are very special indeed. Perhaps the middle age ought to be on the school curriculum along with all other useful life skills, like balancing a budget, coping with change, and resilience. Can you imagine how a class of school children would relate to such an apparently abstract concept as middle age? It would be more cringingly awkward than their sex education classes.

Could it be that people don't want to talk about it? Or is it because we all simply don't know what to say about the middle age? It might be a mixture of both of these things. People might be just too busy surviving their own experiences of parenthood, the trials of work and home life, the 'joy' of new grandparenthood, or newfound freedom in their active retirements. Perhaps they were trying to make sense of it, understand it, or deny it, themselves at the time. How could they possibly help if they were grappling with their own mid-life? Like new parents don't have a baby manual, we don't have benefit of a middle age guide book, not that we should, it would compromise our voyage of discovery. And of course, there is so much rubbish talked about the middle age already. Surely, we all deserve something better now?

My ideas and approach to the middle age aren't about that on their own. They are about living a great life up to that point, living it very well at the moment of middle age, and enjoying and carrying on after that.

Shifting sands.

The middle age is another example of the vagueness and fluidity in the middle. The idea of ageing has been particularly flexible since the advent of teenage and youth culture in the 1950s, and various social and attitudinal shifts throughout the 70 years thereafter, and progressive developments in health care. Looking back, as recently as the 1960s, it was common for you to finish school, get a job, get married, have children. All before 25 years old. By 50, you were most probably a grandparent more than once over, and 10 years or so from official retirement age. There was no doubt then that you were middle aged – was there? After retirement, you weren't expected to live that long either, and it was a period of rest, light grandparenting duties (if there ever is such a thing), and pastimes such as gardening, bowling, or sitting in a working class shed, a middle class conservatory, or an upper class orangery.

My parents fitted that 1960s blueprint. However, in their baby boomer lifetimes, their generation's attitudes have changed significantly and so have their expectations. These were the first mould-breaking teenagers who rejected the conformity of generational expectations and have carried those attitudes throughout their lives. These social shifts and behaviour patterns have to some extent been aided and abetted by improvements in health and wellbeing. Suggest to my mother she was old (at the time of writing in her late-70s) and she would likely chew your head off. Their generation broke the rules at every stage, grabbing hold of the world's opportunities and travel, and embracing active middle age and retirement. They are now *"fated to live lives of full-time leisure. Leisure with a capital L."* said Leicester author Sue Townsend in her book The Public Confessions of a Middle Aged Woman aged 55¾.

It is an issue for all.

All of us have the opportunity to appreciate and value the middle age, because it affects everyone at some point. Whether we are approaching it in the near or distant future, in it at this moment, we are coming out of it on the other side, or if we know someone (in life or work) who is experiencing it now. It is completely and undeniably a matter for every single one of us. I know this because, people do like to talk and think about it - a lot.

My barber, Joe, who I considered to be young (he was in his early thirties then) said he felt middle aged. Bedtime was *"Before 9 o'clock almost always"*, he said. Echoes of Ronald Reagan there I thought, who said: *"Middle age is when you're faced with two temptations, and you choose the one that will get you home by nine o'clock"*. Bedtime shouldn't be a reliable measure, at least I hope not, otherwise, I am doomed. Some people (like me) are morning people, some people prefer the night. It's funny, I merely asked Joe if he thought the Covid-19 lockdown had made us all more middle aged, a great question in hindsight.

Isn't it funny how we construct our own versions of what it means to be middle aged? There are lots of them. I noticed mine and Joe's shared observations of feeling less social, grumpier, and a preference to save money rather than spend it. I didn't even realise until these were behaviours, I considered to be middle aged (interestingly I think these became some of society's post pandemic traits). It was quite a revelation.

Let's organise our thinking.

I'd like you to look at this line. It starts with birth and ends with death. Imagine this line is your life. Now grab that pencil again, and put your mark on it that shows where you think you are on the continuum.

Life ├──────────────────────────────────────┤ **Death**

We shall return to that later, in the meantime we need to look at the numbers. Be warned though, don't be preoccupied with numbers alone, as you may not like the answers you find. However, they are a good starting point.

As usual for everything middling, we need to think about what it is not, so we can rule some things out. To be middle aged, is clearly to be neither young nor old. So, we need to ask the age-old questions of 'how young is young?' and 'how old is old?'. These are very clearly issues of subjectivity, and not objectivity, and therefore out of bounds for polite dinner party conversations. But if we work through these questions, we may start to get closer to the very essence of middle age.

First, let's think about life expectancy. The old adage of 'three score years and ten' set out how long we could reasonably exist until our inevitable death. That's 70 years in new money. 35 was the middle of that, and for generations before the arrival of post World War Two teenage culture, middle age did seem to begin in one's thirties, not long after the responsibilities of marriage and child-rearing.

Nowadays, following medical advances, changes in living conditions and social attitudes, life expectancy is higher in the developed world. According to the UK Office for National Statistics (June 2024) average life expectancy for men was 78.6 years and for women it was 82.6, a slight reduction since the increased death rate during the Covid pandemic, and a gender-neutral average of 80.6 years. In basic maths, half of that is 40.3 years old. Of course, people live shorter or longer lives than the average and reaching 100 years old is by no means a rarity these days. I don't think the middle means half, and so 40 year olds aren't middle aged. So, what other proposals or ideas could we explore?

One idea would be to take childhood out of the question completely and focus on the middle of adult life instead. As adulthood has expanded, so has childhood, and youngpeoplehood (another made up word). Before we disregard it, we need to agree what childhood is. It used to be so much shorter even in my parents' generation. It seemed to end abruptly at 16 years, and whilst a comparatively small minority stayed on at school or went to university, most people went out to work, and accumulated the trappings and responsibilities of adulthood. Some got married (with parental permission). My mum and dad (note I didn't say mother and father, or ma and pa) left school and went straight into work, and they married at 20 and 24 years old. These days, young people are now (required or encouraged to be) in full time education until at least 18 years old. Proportionately many more then go to university, and therefore they start work much later – typically well into their mid-twenties. Whilst various trappings of maturity are phased in legally (like drinking or driving – not together mind), rather than adulthood beginning at the traditional milestones of 18 or 21, it is more like 25 in the twenty-first century. Twenty-fifth birthdays pass by without a ceremony, party, a 'key of the door', or big fuss. We sort of sleepwalk through this new period of transition these days.

With these social and economic shifts, and behavioural or leisure pursuits or choices, our young people are leaving home, forming long-term relationships, and having their own children far later than recent generations. There have been big shifts here even in the past three decades. In 1991, first time mothers were aged 27.7 years old on average in the UK, by 2021 that had moved to 30.9 years old. This phenomenon has been described as the rise of the 'kidult'. Reflecting the difficulties young people experience in leaving their childhood homes, even after university, due to the constraints of student debt, housing costs, and career challenges. The fledglings from the family nest often return on multiple occasions – I call them re-fledglings. This is quite confusing to the empty-nester parent, when they are also grappling with their middle age, and very convenient to those parents who really don't want to let go.

To help us move forward, let's agree then you are a child or young person up to 25 years old. Okay, so that's a quarter of a century already spent on digging and fixing our lifetime foundations. We have been gestated and born, we have toddled, grown and developed, and been educated, we have taken our first steps into the wider world. At which point we are expected to be fully formed adults ready to embrace work and meaningful relationships.

There you have it, the first of what I think could be four 25-year-long quarters in all our life stories. This is what I call the 100 Plan. The boundaries and age definitions aren't set in stone and don't apply to everyone. They act as a guide, to book of life, a volume with four main chapters: starting with birth and foundation, and followed by the second age of adulthood, the third age of middle age, and the fourth age of old age and our inevitable death.

The 100 plan.

Q1	Q2	Q3	Q4
Birth and foundation	**Second age**	**Third age**	**Fourth age**
Gestation ▼ Birth ▼ Childhood ▼ Adolescence	Young adulthood ▼ Adulthood	Middle age	Old age ▼ Death
0-25 years	**25-50 years**	**50-75 years**	**75-100 years**

The expansion of childhood, teenage years, and young adulthood has created a tsunami-like effect upon what we used to consider was being a grown-up adult, our middle age, and old age beyond that. It has sown confusion around what we now call each era of ageing, and what the numbers are.

Next, if we can determine what is old, then we may be on to something. The concepts of childhood and old age can form the bread, and adulthood and the middle age can be the sandwich filling. Expected/average mortality age is certainly a guide to what old may appear to be, but as we will agree no one here wants to be compliantly average. And we understand that some people become older sooner than others. I noticed several of the 70-year-olds I know were most affronted when the government told them they were vulnerable in 2020 – I get why on both sides. My parents complained when the passengers aged in their 70s and 80s were evacuated from a cruise ship, suffering with food poisoning, were described as 'elderly' or 'vulnerable' by BBC news. They were that age and didn't identify as that. We really do need new words for our elders – don't we? But I do consider it reasonable to say the fourth age, is 75 years and older and that contains old age and our goal of mortality.

Not that being old is the same as being dead. I suspect all of this will be much more open to the effects of relativism, and our own concepts of and feelings around it. Many of us consider such debates to be obscene, or distasteful at best, unless you are Jungian of course. He felt death was a transition to a place beyond our knowledge, a goal, and the fulfilment of life's meaning – like a ripe fruit falling from the tree of life.

The perspective of reflection is inevitably influenced by our current position. It is different if we are looking back from a place of safety and happiness, to one of regret and disappointment. This will indelibly colour our experience of the process to come. If you're in a happy place, then the reflection can be nourishing. If you're unhappy and anxious, then a look back can stir all sorts of things up. In either scenario, the possibility of finding a surprise or two (or three) along the way is more than a real prospect. Surprises can appear uninvited whilst you are doing something else, or they can be unearthed by therapy. They can be prompted by physically and virtually bumping into someone. All such events promote certain thoughts, feelings and emotions and bring them to the surface.

Age is much more than a number. My Auntie Sarah once said *"don't EVER tell anyone your age, because that is how people will define you from then on"*. Good advice. Later on, I say the same about revealing your birth order. Sharing such information runs the risk of painting yourself into a corner, with no escape. Limiting self is a wholly unnecessary and fruitless act given we are surrounded by people all too happily queuing up to do that on our behalf. I guess that means the end to big and showy milestone birthday parties. Actor, Dame Joan Collins had something to say as well: *"I never think about age. I believe your age is totally how you feel. I've seen women of thirty-five who are old and people of seventy-five who are young"*. Adding *"I don't look my age, I don't feel my age, and I don't act my age"*. To her, age is just a number. *"It's totally irrelevant unless, of course, you happen to be a bottle of wine"*.

Invaluable ideas Sarah and Joan, and I agree. However, some wine gets better with age, some benefits from early drinking. I agree the middle age cannot, and ought not, be defined simply by a number. When we feel young, middle aged, and old, it must surely be an individual state of consciousness. In short, attitude.

People are interested in looking their age, they say to others, 'ooh you don't look your age?' Which makes me wonder what different ages should look like. We don't know anymore, I am sure of that. As Barbara Royle said, slouched on her sofa watching a travel show, on BBC TV's Royle Family (Series 2, episode 1) *"She's looking her age, though, Judith Chalmers."* *"How old is she?"* asked her daughter Denise. *"Ooh, I don't know."* replied Barbara. A clear illustration of my point. Thank you to the late and great Caroline Ahern for writing that, and to Craig Cash for that matter.

What is left in between is somewhat of an obsession for people. We use each other as mirrors to ourselves. People ask do I look my age? Am I faring better than my friends or siblings? I remember as a child mum pointing at people in the street, before saying *"I was at school with her – can you believe it?"* as she herself triumphantly skipped along the road to congratulate herself on her youthful looks and prove she could still nimbly move.

I hold my hands up. I rarely watch a film without asking how old do you think that actor is? At home, we have a little guessing game and then I Google it. What follows are gasps of disbelief, sniggering giggles, judgemental comments, and occasionally an admiring and congratulatory nod to their good work, or if we compare well ourselves. All in the interests of balance of course.

When I was young, I connected ideas of old age to imminent death. My grandparents always seemed old. They were twice the age of my parents, who also seemed old. That meant my grandparents were in the 50-60 year old range when I arrived and started to grow up and be aware of them. They were still working, but felt ancient to me, and surely close to death I thought. Retirement wasn't far off, indeed in those days pensionable age started at a standard 60 for women, and 65 for men. I imagine that retirement age was much more significant back then and could arguably herald the beginning of old age. But as social attitudes, health, and economics have evolved, then our needs, wants, and choices around pre-retirement, retirement, and post-retirement are much more mercurial. People retire at all sorts of times, earlier, on time, later, or never.

Happy birthday?

US astronaut, John Glenn said there was still no cure for the common birthday. And our reflections and age-related musings are often prompted by our birthdays. Especially those pesky birthdays that end in a big fat zero, an '0'. They come around every once in a while, every ten years actually, and it seems to me that each decade is shorter than the last one. They happen so quickly. I find a birthday with an '0' at the end can make me reflect, and make plans even more than all other birthdays put together. '0' birthdays cause you to look back, look forward and they may prompt a realisation. These '0' birthdays are goal-setting junctions and opportunities. They absolutely make me think about times past and what's been achieved (or not) and to ponder what is still to do, and perhaps contemplate what the future might hold. It is an important thing to do, it is a good distraction in between fending off the inevitable interest and curiosity from those around us, who consider it an invitation for teasing and mockery, or assume it to be a major vicarious feature of their own upcoming social diary.

An '0' birthday is challenging and confronting enough, as a milestone of life. I found it rather easy to reflect on them and pinpoint the age and stage of my life journey. And if not, to indulge in a well-timed distraction of a big party. In addition, I propose it is the middle 5 birthdays that can be more meaningful. They are the pivot points when you look back at the five years past since the last 0 birthday and look ahead to the five years left before the next 0 milestone. As such they are like a micro-middle-age all wrapped up in each decade. And these are especially potent for the middle age in the sixth and seventh decades (the 50s and 60s).

It is the 'Oh' birthdays we all need to worry about. The ones that cause more than the usual life stage reflections. Instead of celebration cakes and balloon-filled parties, they cause a raft of emotional responses of surprise, anger, and disappointment. These aren't good times. The mostly well-meaning but misplaced friendly banter and interest from those around us only serves to make things worse. They feel like verbal assaults. We don't enjoy them, and it only goes to feed dissatisfaction with turning into the next decade. We have the potential to survive getting older and turn it into a positive realisation opportunity. Looking back and resolving, and looking forward to reframe things, can help, so can being present in the present. I recommend building and applying your realisation strategy into your personal business plan. That might sound a little too corporate for you, but I return to personal planning later, and there are many different models to suit your taste.

Of most importance is how you feel and relate to the concepts of age. Having a positive view will help it to be a beneficial experience, like a coat of armour repelling all those ill-advised views. We can self-identify for sure and listen to others as well.

To quote Irish playwright George Bernard Shaw *"Youth, is the most beautiful thing in this world - and what a pity that it has to be wasted on children."* This is frequently mis-quoted and paraphrased, and sometimes credited to another Irish playwright Oscar Wilde. Whoever said it and whenever they did, it nonetheless connects with a tendency to look back at time spent, with a modicum of regret, imagining what different choices we would make if we had that time again. We must not waste too much time on lamenting the passing of youth, with all the trappings and glamour it was supposed to have contained.

That said, now might be a good time to revisit that life timeline.

Life ├──────────┼──────────┼──────────┼──────────┤ **Death**

I wonder where your mark sits alongside these life stage categories, now that we have established the four quarters of the 100 plan. Revisit the line and consider in which quarter you placed yourself. Does that seem right, or are there adjustments to be made in your thinking? Are you a match? Something to think about.

It is time for us to consider the two ages that are adulthood and middle age. For Jung, the period of middle age was one where the soul begins its secret work in getting ready for departure. Once we get to midlife, there is a natural tendency to look backwards as well as forwards. Just like the middle child looking up or down at their older and younger siblings. Or that middle class fellow looking up at his upper class and looking down at his working class contemporaries. Looking back is a great thing to do, as long as it doesn't become an all-consuming activity. This is a time to let go and to live. *"Life can only be understood backwards; but it must be lived forwards"* said Danish theologian Søren Kierkegaard. A good point there. I imagine you may have done just that when revisiting the timeline.

In middle age, we look back to times past and imagine what time remains, and what life will bring. We may conclude more time has passed than remains ahead, and our capacity to make hay is somewhat diminished. Situational pondering is one way we make sense of where we currently are in life, it is that basic instinct of positioning and postulating. A vital enterprise when one finds oneself in the middle, as we are all familiar with now. *"You've got to always go back in time if you want to move forward"* said Snoop Dogg. That middle aged rapper, he's bang on message!

We can romanticise our pasts to such an unrealistic extent we can reinvent them to suit our mood. It fills those moments when we're not working, talking, or aimlessly scrolling through social media on our phones. Maybe it even comes to mind when we're having sex with our current partners. Who doesn't love a little bit of fantasy eh? But it places us in danger of comparing the reinvented and idealised past with what might feel like a lack-lustre present or an unclear, limited or finite future. No one and nothing stands much of a chance against such a freely constructed fantasy. Reality is certainly on the back foot here. That reality being a future of indeterminate length, insecurity, and the unknown.

Maybe the future isn't as comforting as the past, but is something that can be invented and shaped, that is exciting. We must though, be prepared to invest in our futures, take good advice, and move out of our comfort zone once in a while. Even if that just means letting go of old styles and trying a new cut of jeans – as long as it is the right ones of course. Ones that suit, fit, and are age and stage appropriate. We notice the things that we have lost and consider the future limitations - the things we don't or can't do anymore, like fit into 30-inch waist jeans, get up from a chair in silence, immediately remember someone's name, sleep all night without waking up or needing to go to the toilet, or sing along to recent music releases. It's a time when health commonly becomes a key consideration *"When you begin to exchange your emotions for symptoms"* said Georges Clemenceau, the former French prime

"You've got to always go back in time if you want to move forward."

———○———

Snoop Dogg

minister. Indeed, in middle age, I challenge you to try and have a whole conversation with someone without talking about aches and pains.

Looking at the past can be the easiest option, there is probably more to look at – and it is a known fact – in the main (we can do odd things with what we remember and how we interpret events). The past is bigger and longer (at least when you are middle aged), it is definite and known. Like in any history, there are several versions of the truth, 'recollections vary'. We cannot even trust ourselves to remember the correct versions of the past. Some things may need picking apart to make greater sense. The risk for many is that looking back can uncover feelings of unfinished business, difficult times, trauma, regret, and/or unfulfilled dreams. Sometimes such recollections can come like bolts out of the blue. This can be unsettling and all consuming. *"A man is not old until regrets take the place of dreams"* said actor John Barrymore.

Everyone has something to say.

One thing that is different about the middle age, compared to the other middles, is that lots of people, not just comedians, have lots to say about it. There's no shortage of quotes, I have peppered some of them unapologetically throughout this chapter: comedians, politicians, 'first ladies', presidents, rappers, religious figures, social leaders, feminists, authors – they all have something to say.

The issue of middle age regularly attracts the attention of magazine editorial. They mainly take a clichéd or an irreverent tone and rely upon the findings of relatively thin, and mostly corporately sponsored research from pension or cruise ship companies. What's more there's a sneaky insinuation hiding behind them, the suggestions are time is running out and/or a midlife crisis is not far off, or one is happening already simply by judgements placed on various lifestyle choices. I read one recently and was surprised at their finding the middle aged are happy to invest in quality cutlery and crockery. Not something I would disagree with, being a homewares retailer on the side, but I was a little startled at the apparent randomness of the assertion. Until I discovered the survey was funded by a quality cutlery and crockery supplier. Go figure. That survey said middle age started at 47 years. The Healthspan survey in 2021 concurred, although they said for men it was 48, and for women it was 45. In 2021, Generation Zs in a survey by Perspectus Global, the US tech company, said it started at 45 years old.

Other people aside, your body is talking to you. I like Bob Hope's quote, despite it being humorous. It's great to have an obvious physical and measurable definition of a middle – for a change. And it is one that resonates very much with me. I am no stranger to watching the ebb-and-flow of my own middle. Middle age spread is the reason why food and exercise has to be part of my week, and for very many of us over the age of forty. As I often say, 'it takes a lot of work to look this average'. It really does. When one reaches this age, there is a great deal of effort required to manage diet, health, weight, and fitness. Gone are the days of eating whatever you want or being able to effortlessly run for the bus. Middle life takes applied effort and preparation. And I urge everyone to not shirk this duty to self, wellbeing, and body. We can reject the temptation to think middle aged spread is an inevitable experience of the middle age. Too many people I observe seem to surrender to these physical forces and give up at this stage. They seem oblivious to their morbid self-harm and give in to instant gratification. *"After 30, your body has a mind of its own"* Anonymous. That is true, but it means we need to consciously take over so we can counter its objective. It is time to be mindful about it. On the flipside, many do make conscious efforts to become or maintain fitness. The 'fit-at-fifties' are lifting weights to counter their depleting hormones. Good on them.

For me, in the middle age the body is giving an outward sign of change and that something isn't working and needs adjusting. We should all listen to our bodies and tackle this head on. It won't be easy, but it is necessary. *"Thirty-five is when you finally get your head together and your body starts falling apart"* said Caryn Leschen, the editor in chief of Wimmin's Comix, the influential all-female underground comics anthology. Unless you do something about it, that is.

As well as your body, your conscious and unconscious mind is also talking to you. We often look back at our connections with friends and family, and significant relationships, whether they be short- or long-term ones. These are the echoes of our unfinished business and past encounters. What about that partner that you let slip, or left too soon, or separated from untidily, or still hold affection for? Were there words left unsaid? Were there things said you would like to finish, take back, or explain? In middle age there is time to ponder the 'what ifs'. What if something hadn't happened, or instead what might have become if something else had? Those bends of destiny, happy coincidences, and chance encounters. They play with our minds and enter our dreams or our therapy sessions.

Using a process to process.

The death of one's youth is being grieved in the middle age, at the same time we start to prematurely grieve our own demise – whenever that will occur. Like any grieving process it will follow the phases identified by Elisabeth Kubler-Ross, a Swiss-American psychiatrist who worked with the terminally ill, in her 1969 book, On Death and Dying. Once considered as revolutionary, her theories have since been rejected as overly simplistic. Why complicate matters, I say? Her theories help us pinpoint the feelings of shock and denial, anger and frustration, bargaining, depression and acceptance in processing endings. And any transition from one age-era in life to another is an ending as well as a beginning. Our individual journeys through these processes are just that, individual. Some of the stages we visit fleetingly, others can stick to us like limpets and barnacles. A midlife moment of realisation can be a colossal personal shock. It may cause a chain reaction that stimulates the process of grief and loss and kick-start those sequential stages.

1. Shock and denial.

We need to recognise when middle age is happening. It is common for this process to take quite some time, and to be spread across a series of small incremental steps. Please don't fall into the trap of thinking they hit you altogether at 100 miles an hour. They rarely do. Instead, they gradually creep up, you don't notice, or you subconsciously or consciously deny or ignore it. That is until that tipping point moment when a jigsaw puzzle picture has formed and you can see it in its totality (or someone else tells you what they can see).

We all need to be better at seeing the middle age coming. The problem is we can be all too easily distracted with our early life, early adulthood, adulthood, careers and families - all these things in various combinations. With all this busyness we neglect to appreciate the inevitability of our middle age is approaching and we do little to prepare for it – emotionally or physically. There's benefit in horizon scanning, no matter how busy or whatever age we are.

This can be very frustrating. These feelings though, if not accepted, spent well, shared, or healthily processed are certainly the recipe for a bout of depression. Then we may enter a stage of panic-ridden experimentation – those things like new relationships, new hairstyles, or fashion choices. We might walk into a clothes store that we haven't visited for 20 years. We might 'borrow' fashion styling from our children – much to their utter (and completely justifiable) horror.

Decisions as I have said are key – only with good advice or benefit of a sounding board. And then, with a following wind we can reach our new direction, integrated into our sense of being and wellbeing.

With any change, ending, or unexpected event(s), there can be a sense of unreality that inhibits our ability to accept truth or actuality. Our sense of denial helps us to manage or cope with the loss and to survive our initial shock. We say to ourselves: 'this cannot be true', 'I don't believe it', 'there must be a mistake'. And so, in the example of the loss of youth, or entry into middle age, or old age after that, this can cause a denial of one's age or stage of life, and a clinging on to things that have passed their use-by-date. Some are gripping the door frame and are refusing to come in. There is a common desire for some to delay middle age. And it is one of the most frequently deployed coping mechanisms. Rather than tackling an issue, coming to terms with it, let's delay it instead no matter how superficially.

To move through this phase needs some acceptance, and a plan to deal with what is to come.

2. Anger.

Anger is a wide-ranging set of behaviours, most often characterised by aggressive physical or verbal outbursts, sometimes with the intent to harm others, and rarely with good outcomes. It can be passive where the person ruminates and internalises their anger, avoiding it by distracting themselves, again something not good for the long-term. Such behaviours can be directed at oneself, friends, family, employers or even random strangers. The middle, and my preferred way, is an assertive approach, where there is an active engagement with the anger and its triggers, with the use of clear and specific (non-provocative) communication through good negotiation of what is needed to accept the grief. Opportunities for people to discharge their emotional and physical energy are important here, whether that be at work or at leisure. In short, let it out, let it go. Move on.

3. Bargaining.

Then we run the risk of becoming strangely irrational. We attempt to reverse the change, ending, or death (or at least its impact). This is the bargaining stage. We cannot bring people back to life, but we might want to reclaim our youth for example, by surrounding ourselves with younger people, or adopting the behavioural or fashion characteristics of them, changing partner even. The usefulness of this process is it can offer us hope, a reduction of the pain and suffering, and grow the belief that something better will come next. Poor bargaining choices can have catastrophic consequences and must be carefully considered. At the time of writing, it is believed that we cannot turn back time.

4. Depression.

Unfortunately, there is a moment of acceptance when it becomes abundantly clear that most, if not all, of our bargaining behaviours don't work. We come to realise they will never succeed in reversing what has happened, is happening, or will happen. This is the stage that most people understand and relate to. Mostly, we all understand the notion of deep sadness, emotional exhaustion, and misery. This stage of depression may be brief. However, it could be long lasting and damaging. All of us can benefit from support and positive strategies to manage depression and our swift journey out of it. This is when the long-term choices need to be made. Let me be frank, beyond all that reflection on what could have been, and after all that fantasy and flirting, the middle age can be an extremely challenging, distressing, and difficult time. You are bobbing along thinking about other things, and then you realise things aren't right, or at least different to how they used to be. That moment in life can suddenly feel disappointing, directionless, or just plain dull. That's the recipe for a 'crisis' of confidence, triggering questions about your very existence and purpose, and a sense of dread about an apparently directionless future. If this is you or a friend, help is needed.

5. Acceptance.

Finally, and at the point of time that is right for you, the reality of the situation and your physical and emotional self ultimately accepts the situation, and does something useful about it. That doesn't mean the shadows of denial, anger, bargaining, and depression disappear, they may revisit from time to time, like the ebb and flow of the tide. It means things are more tolerable, more routine, and normalised. Life goes on. You can move on – with a plan. You can find joy.

"Age is an issue of mind over matter. If you don't mind, it doesn't matter."

———○———

Mark Twain

Realisation not crisis.

The term midlife crisis is a modern construct, attributed by some to the psychologist Elliot Jacques in 1965, according to Psychology Today. In creating the term, Jacques described the tussle of the reckoning with one's own mortality. There are similarities with depression because at this stage there can be a loss of interest in the usual things or routines of life, a general lowness, this can soon become all consuming. A bad day can be just that, it needn't turn onto a bad week, a dreadful month, or indeed a terrible year. That said, it could be the start of an existential predicament – a loss of all hope. In which case it could be a depression, and help may be needed.

I reject the term crisis. I am ripping out that page, screwing it up into a tight ball, and throwing it into the bin. Instead, I prefer to describe these moments as 'realisations'. That is much more positive, and for me it much more accurately describes what is going on. This is a moment of realising one's current age and stage in life and responding emotionally to it. It is the beginning of thinking about acceptance and what you want next out of life.

Of course, a realisation might not be anything to worry about, or to consider too much. Like US writer Mark Twain said: *"Age is an issue of mind over matter. If you don't mind, it doesn't matter"*. You can always rely on Mr Twain to nail a quote.

What's happening in middle age 'realisation' is we are being pulled in two different directions. It is like that transitional period between childhood and teenage years. When one wants the sanctuary and simplicity of childhood, yet one yearns for the magnetic new adventures, freedom, and challenges of teenage adolescence. In the middle age we are being pulled and tempted back to our younger days, whilst attempting to fend off or deny our older selves, as reluctant participants in the ageing process. It is a split position. *"Middle age is that perplexing time of life when we hear two voices calling us, one saying, 'why not?' and the other, 'why bother?'"* said the journalist and columnist

Sidney J Harris. We could instead be embracing the now, whilst accepting our ageing selves.

If a powerful realisation does happen to you, it could be the catalyst for making good decisions about what happens next. Easier said than done, I know. Keep reading, I will set out a framework to help later. A realisation is a 24-carat opportunity to recognise how you got there, to the middle age, to fully understand it, to process lessons learned, and to let go of the things that aren't useful for you anymore. With this insight and freedom, you have the opportunity to move forward through this next exciting phase of life, and for that matter the one after that. A phase that I must admit I struggle to label. Is it post-middle-age or the-new-old, or just old age? But that's something for later. For now, we all need some good advice and support to manage the middle. So, what is it?

I was speaking with a friend, he was in his late forties. He was talking about his confused and mixed feelings about his age and stage of life. *"I'm not having a midlife crisis"* he asserted, whilst casting me a sideways glance to check if I was going to believe him, reassure him, agree, or come to a different conclusion. I must admit, I was doing all of that. We settled on the positive thought there was a midlife 'reflection' going on. That said, this was one-and-a-half years into the global COVID-19 pandemic, and anyone can be forgiven for feeling low and succumbing to wide ranging and questioning thoughts about the past, present, future, and mortality at that time. He said he wasn't looking back in regret; things weren't better when he was younger, and he was looking forward to a better and brighter future full of new adventures. Maybe then there was an impatience, prompted by a finite sense of time ahead, and an apparent urgency to get on with that lifetime that was left. Something constrained incredibly powerfully by the punitive effects of the pandemic. *"It feels like I am in a rut, and we are all in a globally enforced rut. I know I need to keep positive"* he said. It certainly is time to review life so far and the present, reconcile the past and shed any unnecessary baggage, and reason i.e. goal and objective set for what happens next. We must keep hold of the power to determine our own destinies, and not submit to global forces constructed by those who wish us to comply with their grand plans.

Acceptance.

Given it is a relatively new idea, it is no wonder that we have yet to reach peace and a sensible relationship with the middle age. It takes time for us all to adjust as a society and as individuals. Much longer than we might realise. And our approach to middle age has been under constant attack by some very powerful social forces – humour, mockery, unhelpful help, and changing attitudes to age and its acceptable and unacceptable boundaries. Life in modern times is fast moving and fast changing. That means we need to adjust and readjust regularly. Our definition of the middle age needs to change regularly.

Like when we try to make sense of class, we need to apply the objective, subjective, and relational measures. These can be unreliable and problematic – but they do offer some help and guidance. A big message is that we need to anticipate and plan for the middle age, not considering our approach, or arrival for that matter, into middle age as an end, but a milestone instead. And as such we have a wonderful opportunity to take control of it. If we have a good plan, then we can reboot our lives, be leaders of our own internal revolution, be our own personal reinventors.

It truly is an opportunity to build your own renaissance. Don't be too hasty to enter it though, seductive as it might be. There is no rush, it will come soon enough. And on the flipside, don't leave it until it is too late either. It is yours for the taking.

I feel we have the chance to do more to celebrate being middle age on a more regular basis. You've survived youth, you are a grown up, and you've a plan for what is happening next. What could be better than that?

The retirement revolution.

I 'ummed and ahhed' about including a section on retirement in this chapter. But I think it is the right thing to do. The middle age is a pre-retirement phase for some, or it is the time when people do retire, or embrace a new phase in their lives or work. They might reduce work hours or change to part-time, as a phased-in retirement approaches. The expansion and contraction of the different phases in our lives from childhood and beyond all require us to think again about what we want and need from retirement.

I was thrilled recently to spend time with an ex-colleague who had retired over 10 years ago. It was lovely to welcome her back to acknowledge her contribution to our business on its anniversary, and to reconnect with other ex-colleagues. What struck me, however, was the words and reactions from those other colleagues. I first started to notice this when three or four times I overheard the phrase 'I would be bored if I retired'. That got me thinking.

Now, I love to work. I really do. And I have to be creative. But given the choice I might not work at all, I would work less, or at least differently – perhaps on other projects. I look forward to when my work is done at the end of every day and each week. Because when work ends, play begins. My professional self becomes the personal me. I can garden, cook, read, write, travel, volunteer, study, or spend more time with family and friends – and make some new ones. Or do nothing. Who wouldn't want more time to do any of that?

What a strange state-of-affairs to think you would be bored without work when there is so much more to do in life. And I know my retired ex-colleague has a very full, vital and active life without work. I admire her for that. I started to wonder if those who think they'd be bored without work, are bored now when they are in work. Have they lost track of themselves and who they really are beyond the workplace?

Now, there have been times in my life when work has got in the way of life, I have had work-life imbalance and I have suffered. I hadn't had the time to pursue all other interests. But those days are long gone – thankfully. If people are thinking retirement isn't for them, I wonder if there is imbalance in their work and life now? Or is work their play? Are they fearful there will be an imbalance in retirement?

For many, they cannot afford to retire in the ways we have traditionally come to understand, state pensions are starting later and later, and pensions are not always available or sufficient. Is the self-worth gained from income generation too seductive for some that they find it impossible to let go of? Is the end of wage or salary earning, the death of a career, too potent a sign of imminent demise?

Whatever, there are boundary issues for me. I think it is vital we have boundaried work and life identities. I have not met anyone in their later years who told me they wished they had worked more. Indeed, they say the opposite.

Like many others, I am not a fan of the term. Retirement literally means to withdraw from life. When my time comes, I will not be doing that. I might be withdrawing from work or starting something new. It could be the time I take up an alternative or new work activity or a volunteering role. It could be more study or writing another book. Some would call that work. I know that doesn't sound like a traditional retirement – to stop work and then start again. But this is the new reality of 'retirement', one where people have more they want to achieve for themselves or to contribute to their communities. This is a massive shift from how things were when I was a child; have one career, stop work at 60 or 65, and do seemingly very little afterwards. Now it is more about phased and different careers, two or three of them for each of our work lifetimes and another in your retirement. It may be the occupation is more time to spend with family and friends, or to travel.

Rather than retirement, we're increasingly adopting a 'protirement' (yep, another one of my made-up words). This is a combination of proactive and retirement, reflecting the idea of proactivity and positively rather than passive recoiling or deficit. In mine, I am determined I will not be idle or bored, and there will be plenty of time and space for new things. I will have worked and thought too hard to settle for anything less.

Improving with age?

No one, and I mean no one, says 'you look middle aged' and considers it to be a compliment. Perhaps it boils down to simple vanity – if there is such a thing. Yesterday I had a Zoom call with someone I had known for over 25 years. I was in my twenties when we met. Even though we had been in touch, I hadn't seen her for the last 10 years. Now I'm middle aged. She said I hadn't changed a bit. How rude. I thought I'd improved, like a good wine!

We commonly say some people are middle aged before their time, or at least early, or before anyone else. I wondered what signs and symptoms might be present for us to reach such a judgement. I think there may be attitudinal or behavioural characteristics, or symbols of style or fashion (or the lack of it). Is it therefore possible to be middle aged in your twenties, I wonder? Or are we talking about early ageing here? That is an idea that raises health and economic equalities we ought to consider. We often hear the phrase, being old before your time. As if that is a bad thing. It all seems so old-fashioned and clichéd doesn't it? We will all be happier if we view the middle age and ageing as positive things and live in their present rather than being avoidant and disparaging. I guess, for some people it starts earlier, and for some others it starts later. For me, I think middle age comes soon enough and is beyond your control. And so, I wouldn't recommend rushing into it. We cannot all be average and robotically switch from one of our age-eras to another. But crucially, when you are there, you need to be ready for it, and to make the most of it, because before we know it, we will be leaving middle age and entering old age.

Try these alternatives.

Prevention is better than cure. But when things get tough, it is good to focus on what is okay, what luck you have, and the things to be optimistic about. This can all form a solid foundation for moving what needs to change.

-Let's celebrate the middle age.

We are all in desperate need to unashamedly celebrate the middle age. I know there is a gender issue here. Men are much more likely to benefit from the authority, power, and wealth accumulated up to this point of life. For women, the coinciding of middle age with the effects of the menopause has the power to double down on the disadvantages. I fully acknowledge that.

The middle age really is something to cherish for all of us. Let's celebrate it before it is too late. Life is short, and the ticking of time carries on at an alarming and unstoppable pace. The best advice is don't delay, do it straightaway. As actor and singer Doris Day once pointed out *"The really frightening thing about middle age is the knowledge that you'll grow out of it"*.

-Find the happiness.

For me, the midpoint of life is bookmarked when one notices the future is becoming smaller and defined, when once it felt infinite.

The middle age can be a golden time. Maybe even a chance to take a breath. You have hopefully made it through the trials and tribulations of childhood and adolescence, and early adulthood with only a few battle scars. If so, well done.

The middle is a time when life could be a little easier and lighter, a life stage informed by the lessons learned along the way. By making sense of it we increase our chances of making it a good time. A 25-year study by Alberta University found a growth in levels of happiness from the early twenties. Their hypothesis was the older we got, the happier we became. Enjoy Yourself (It's Later Than You Think) sang The Specials. They knew youth was fleeting and their message was enjoy first whilst not forgetting to gain wisdom, knowledge and understanding along the way: *"enjoy yourself while you're still in the pink"*.

It can though be a time that exposes a sense of deep unhappiness.

"The really frightening thing about middle age is the knowledge that you'll grow out of it."

---○---

Doris Day

-Repair and recover.

If the wounds are deep, let's repair them as quickly and effectively as possible for the reasons explained above. The echoes of all our pasts can be guiding and helpful forces, not ones that scream and shout negativity or throw limitations at us. Regretfully, and all too often, those lessons aren't learned enough, old habits are hard to break and lessons aren't always applied at all. By sorting out and letting go of the unhelpful baggage carried to this point forward, you can progress onwards without it weighing you down further. That's why every middle aged person needs a plan.

-Good housekeeping: Tying up loose ends.

In young adulthood and later, life can be full, fast, and packed with distractions, dreams, temptations, and new opportunities. It is easy to feel relationships didn't start or finish well, or events were chaotic or untidy. Looking back in middle age prompts many questions. What if things had been different? Another door could have opened, a train may have been missed (watch the 1998 movie Sliding Doors if you haven't already), other choices taken – or not. What if we had said yes more often than we said no? Or no more often than we said yes.

All these scenarios can all wriggle around like brain-worms in our consciousness and subconsciousness. They will appear in your dreams in one way or the other, as the 'could've beens', or the unfinished business or sentences. All very disconcerting.

-Positively reframe the narrative.

We are in desperate need to change the narrative, laugh less, and talk about the middle age better; to rebrand and reboot it. I have trawled various articles, all concerning themselves with the middle age. It is surprising how many have taken lazy approaches and listed so-called signs of middle age. And guess what? It's all mocking, negative, or about loss (not gain) – well mostly. And that simply does not fit with the aim of this book, we must positively reframe all of those right here, right now.

There are themes around losing touch, or not keeping up with things like the latest technology which fails to acknowledge the held abilities to operate all sorts of tech that preceded it. Naturally, different generations have different everyday language, and whilst the middle aged are called out for not knowing the latest lingo, their wider, richer, and deeper language is overlooked.

Then there are the signs of physical deterioration like feeling stiff, being unable to rise from a chair without a groan, or taking an afternoon nap (because you can). Even though there is a chance that stiffness was caused by pushing physical boundaries at the gym or in the garden. There is a health theme, especially talking about health more, no doubt due to being more aware, proactive, and focused on managing health – and not taking it for granted.

Then there is memory loss, or slower memory recall (things like people's names). I say older people know more and the back catalogue of all that data is huge, so why wouldn't it take a while? Maybe you are realising these people aren't that interesting, or memorable, and you'd rather focus on other priorities. I'm more than happy to forget unnecessary things if it opens capacity to learn new things or meet new people. Maybe they didn't tell you their names in the first place. Perhaps you didn't ask, or you're established middle class and call everyone 'dahling'.

-Being out and about.
We are told the middle aged are less sociable, preferring a night in rather than a night out in noisy bars or restaurants, instead wanting to spend quality time with favourite friends and family. This is completely understandable if you've found that sexy person you want to be with, and this way you'll get into bed with them quicker, without spending unnecessary funds on an overly expensive drink, food, and taxi, courtship ritual like younger people have to invest in.

When the middle aged go out, then behaviours can become a problem, for others that is, when they don't appreciate feedback, views and opinions, or complaints. People need to better value such assertiveness rather than wince in its presence. This is why middle aged people prioritise spending time with people who have open minds and understand the nature of reasonable debate. On one condition, the views expressed need to be reasonable, non-judgemental, and well-informed.

-Don't deny it.
To deny middle age is to delay it, out of annoyance or disbelief at its approach, and is a missed opportunity. There is a tremendous fear of the middle age and what comes next, of being older than that, and/or contemplating life's purpose, and the eventuality of death. It really is a ticking time bomb. There is an understandable sense of being out of control or running out of time. There can be a strong temptation to want to turn the clock back and counter the forces of nature. Like the Viking King Canute proved, not even the ruling elite can stop the tide.

The methods deployed here are depressingly predictable: fashion revamps (black leather jacket), restyling hair or purchasing some (hair that is), adopting new cultural habits, hanging out with much younger people, buying a red convertible sports car, plastic surgery, other questionable purchases and so on. Many activities facilitated by drawing down tax-free pension funds, another cruel twist of fate at this life-stage crossroads. New hobbies emerge, things like financial and pension planning, changing work hours, pondering (and closely monitoring) retirement timescales (I know lots of people who can tell you how many years, months, days and hours they have until R-day – with only a moment's notice), paying off mortgages, managing the separation from grownup offspring, and coordinating elder care. Not everyone is so fortunate to have such choices, and all of this (or none of this) can fuel uncertainty and anxiety.

-Help a friend who might be struggling.
We all have a great responsibility if and when we notice our friends, family, partners, or colleagues displaying the signs of a midlife struggle. In these situations, we can listen to them, to what they are

saying, and what they are not telling us. Focus on their feelings, reflect back what they are saying and how they are feeling. Consider how is it making you feel as this may give you a clue and help you connect with their true feelings. Don't seek easy distractions, or defences to make you feel less awkward, or plunge into the depths of unhelpful humour. Don't rush to rescue, take action, or propose solutions either – they don't need rescuing, they need acknowledging. Don't tell them what to do. But perhaps be there to catch them if they fall or start making the erroneous decisions or choices.

-Take control of your middle age.
Get help from others. You need to talk about it, to someone or some people who will be helpful, whether that be your partner, friends, family, doctor or therapist. At this point, we need to make good choices. Selecting the right source of support is a tricky prospect. Self-help is an option, but some of us cannot and must not be trusted to do this on our own. Because our stress response could be triggered and we may freeze (get stuck in our lives), fight (create conflict and tension and prompt all sorts of drama) or flight (run away, leave, or avoid). There are real risks - that we will choose to take up unhealthy habits, have an affair or two, leave the family, or seek out new thrills and spills. Or even worse, choose jeans that don't suit you.

Set a future path. A new positive direction needs to be based upon a number of sensible conditions. Yes, we can be sensible whilst seeking out new adventures. Trust me. First, acknowledge these feelings are natural and normal. You aren't the first to feel this way. And second, feelings are not instructions. By that I mean, just because you feel trapped it doesn't mean you escape and run for the hills. Just because you feel time is running out, it doesn't mean it is, and you need to panic. Or just because you feel your relationship isn't what you want, it doesn't mean you leave it. Change it, by changing yourself first instead. But how?

Unfortunately, the confusion of confidence in midlife can cause many to seek the unhealthy validation of others. That is code for saying some seek out flirtations, one-night-stands, affairs or new or rekindled relationships that cause the end of marriages or partnerships.

We can benefit from taking a good hard look at ourselves, and the lives we are living. This self-reflection is better sooner rather than later. We mustn't lose sight of ourselves through the distractions of work, child rearing, or anything else.

Creating a new positive direction needs to be based on also identifying the things to be grateful for. Balance out the problems and feelings that are poking at your conscience. What are the good things that are also in your life? And keep talking about all of it to whomever you have chosen. And talk to yourself, write things down in your diary or journal or blog (public or private). Goals need to be growth based and not deficit models. By that I mean they can be about adding not taking away, being positive and nourishing and developmental, not punitive or negative. Goals need to be realistic too. These new choices need to be respectful and thankful to you and all those around you: Build, don't raze your life to the ground. Extend your life, don't abandon it. Remember that change is good. Calm down. There really is no need to be so dramatic. There's no need for a crisis.

1. **Notice it.**
2. **Value it.**
3. **Make positive choices.**
4. **Create your purposeful direction.**

A business plan for you.

There's much to do in middle age, so we can improve its many aspects and prospects. It is important we invest in our health, wellbeing, and set out our future plans. Because middle age requires, no demands us, to be more than a little determined and to apply conscious and deliberate effort. I advocate we all need a plan, and helpful things in the diary to achieve that plan.

I remember that pivotal point, my pre-middle age period, when I started to think middle age was about to become my reality. I had spent so much time growing my business, then, around 40, I realised that an equal amount of determined effort and investment in myself was not only desirable, it was essential. I was right. Without it, my physicality, my middle, my wellbeing, my ability to cope with pressure, my attitude to change, and my resilience would be a shadow of what it is today. By having my plan I was ready, willing, and able to tackle my middle age – and others middles for that matter.

The activities such a plan contains need to be built into your daily and weekly routines. They need to be in your diary, on your calendar. For me, that's how things get done.

There are lots of templates to be found. Some in books, and there's plenty online. Many models are far too corporate and emotionally unintelligent in my view, although I have found some useful headings:

A few words about business planning for those not used to it. This is a plan based on what you want to happen, with achievable steps towards realistic goals. Plans are your best estimate. But plans change, and so can you. You need to be prepared to change the plan, up or down, based on how you are progressing. Treat it like a good guide or friend to help you gain and retain focus. And whatever you do, celebrate your achievements and successes along the way. If it helps, write monthly, weekly or daily lists. A big review like this need only happen when you feel it necessary, maybe once a year or so.

Plan.

Health.

An obvious concern and foundation is your physical and emotional wellbeing.

Build in actions around managing and responding to past and present health.

To help future health take preventative action through diet and exercise appropriate to your age and stage of life.

(Fill in)

Family and friends.

A good social life is vital. Family and friends are a heady mix of past, present, future relationships, and responsibilities.

Your business plan can set out the time and investment you need to spend and make, and what you hope to get in return.

An audit may reveal the people in your social circle who aren't good for you, or who you could reorganise or recategorise.

Relationships.

Relationships are important, and they need to be nourishing.

Every plan should feature solid, supportive and rich relationships with others. Even if it is with the dog.

It is entirely possible and acceptable to have a business plan for self that doesn't require you to be in a relationship, whether that be a short-, medium- or long-term one.

Learning.

We've heard about the importance of learning in the nourishment of life and feeling good about oneself.

There can always be something in your plan that is about learning something new.

It need not be a PHD in neuroscience, or a degree. It could be a new recipe, a new dance move, or reading a new book.

Plan.

Fun and recreation.

Let's not be too serious. There's plenty of time to have fun. But fun is a serious business.

Having fun isn't always a spontaneous activity, it needs to be something you plan for, and allow time for.

Go on, let go, as often as you can.

Business, career, work, or retirement.

You may not work, but if you do, consider your goals and aspirations whilst you are there.

It is important to consciously consider what and who you want to be at work or in retirement – and why.

There are always opportunities to think about what you can take control of beyond what you are being told to do by others.

(Fill in)

Finances.

Finances can form the bedrock of feelings of anxiety and despair, or they can offer you freedom and control.

Some people love to manage their finances, some hate it. Whatever, finances are something you cannot ignore. Get help if you need to.

Time.

Time seems to be flying by at a rate of knots and is one thing we cannot control.

Filling your time with new and different experiences does help to create a sense or feeling of slowing time down.

Balancing that with time to rest and recover, to stay in, go to bed earlier, get up later, say no, and embrace the JOMO (the joy of missing out).

All of these categories are useful. But on the face of it, you could develop quite a dull plan. What makes the killer difference is another six questions that really can release your powers of personal business planning. For all those sections above, you could be thinking about the following:

1. What can I let go of?

- The things that aren't good for you.
- What you need to let go of.
- Feeling able to let go of these things.
- Actions to help make this happen.

2. What needs to be worked out and processed?

- The difficult things that are troubling you.
- The thoughts you are preoccupied with.
- Unfinished business.
- Working things out through self-help, sharing with someone, talking about, or receiving some counselling or therapy?

3. How can I invest in my emotional self?

- Taking time and effort to invest in your emotional development.
- Being prepared for the process to be uncomfortable and challenging, before it gets better.

4. How can I invest in my physical self?

- Actions that invest in your physical development and health.
- Being prepared for actions to be uncomfortable and challenging for longer term gains.
- Ensuring you nourish yourself.

5. What can I let in?

- Who and what you will let into your life.
- Who you are going to connect with, share with, and live your life with.
- What you are going to eat or drink, or not.

6. What can I give out?

- The things you are going to give out to the world around you.
- The ways in which you are going to give or help others.
- Knowing your gifts, time, care, attention, support, or money or something else.
- Being bold enough to give first, to make the first move.

You've re

mia

...ched the

dle

Reaching our own understanding.

On reflection, I can see how the time up to my mid twenties was my childhood, youth, and foundation. After then and up to my late forties was a consolidation period, a phase that ended in pre-middle age preparations. Since then, my life had flown and the fruit on my vine has matured. It has felt like a golden time, like the warmth of the early afternoon of life.

It was in my 56th year, whilst writing this book, when I felt middle aged truly and deeply. It was a year when I sold my business, adopted a new role at work (in middle management as it happens), noticed more how people were treating me differently in society and at work, and my father died. A busy and eventful year, and I most definitely had a sense I was in the mid-afternoon and it was time for tea. I received a birthday card that quoted the US comedian Phyllis Diller *'I'm at an age when my back goes out more than I do'*. I had a bad back at the time. It hurt when I laughed.

Final thoughts.

I have quickly found the middle age, like the middle classes is that space between two different things. In the middle age, you're too old to be called young, and you're too young to be called old. If you don't feel young and you don't feel old, that could mean you are middle aged.

I have found we need to better and more deeply understand the middle age. We need to plan for it, enjoy it when we get there, and help everyone around us now and in the future to do the same. That would be a great legacy to leave for future generations.

Like starting pension investments, you are never too young to start considering your middle age. If you are in it – it's not too late to make your own changes and choices either. And you are never too old to adopt the best bits of it either, even if you think middle age is very much a thing of the past. Be more middle I say. Always and forever.

We all have the power to avoid that traditional 'midlife crisis', they are not, I repeat not, inevitable. If you are in one, you can turn it around and navigate yourself or your friends out of it. Realisation can be a result of simply having time to think about our life point and how it fits within the past and the future. It can be caused by an impactful self-development experience, or one of those life jolting episodes – like a flippant comment from a 'friend', or any one of the following: life, career or work dissatisfaction; unhappiness in marriage or relationships (or lack of them); health issues, worries or difficulties; the death or serious illness of a friend, close relative, or parent; the occurrence of an '0' birthday or an 'Oh' birthday; becoming a grandparent; or any change at work. All of these can prompt depression and/or a potent sense of time running out – that there is less time ahead than there is behind you. Emotionally, you may feel trapped or stilted. You may not like what you see in the mirror.

We really do need to look beyond the laughter and reject ill-informed narratives, and search harder and deeper for more useful advice and guidance. Do the maths if you must, but reach your own conclusions based on how you feel, and only listen to useful people. I recommend you choose your favourite quotes(s) and use them regularly as affirmations to help you accept the middle age. But that is just the start. Plan and invest in positive actions and put that plan and budget into action. As part of that plan, ensure you celebrate and enjoy your middle age at all times. To do that you may need to tackle things that are holding you back and are filling up your time with unnecessary blocks or distractions from the joy of middle age. Then, when all that is sorted, you need to prepare yourself for what comes next.

—o—

The middle child

"Very often us middle children find ourselves as bridges."

——○——

**Liza Tarbuck,
BBC Radio presenter.**

Getting started.

Some babies are born or brought into families first, others are born or brought in last. Some find themselves in the middle, whether they were born, brought in, or blended into a family. After that, they are forever known as middle children.

There was an estimated 70 million in the US alone (according to Salmon 2012). Given that fact, it is surprising there is so little written about middle children. Much that I have found isn't that great (with a few notable exceptions). Too much though has been really depressing and unimaginative.

Middle children are not well understood. They have the reputation for being ill-fitting, awkward siblings, lurking in the shadows of others. This is both unkind and unnecessary. There are positive qualities, of course there are. Because, even if you feel as a second or other child (even a first), that there was any parenting deficit or societal pre-judgment, we can positively concentrate on how that may have helped us all later in life and made us who we are today.

And if people are chattering about middle born children, there is a massive tendency to be negative and to perpetuate generation-held myths and stereotypes. The story is that middle children are ignored, unsure of their place, unambitious, or disgruntled at their middling position. Like all things middle, the middle child is mostly described by what they are not – rather than what they are. They are not the oldest, nor the youngest child. There is an enormous tendency for people to judge middle children, to put them in a box, or to paint them into a corner. And that is a big problem, if you are that middle child, a sibling, or a parent of one. This dearth of useful information and all this unhelpful discourse is doing us all a disservice. It isn't helping middle children, their siblings, parents, grandparents and extended families, or their life partners. Neither is it useful for their peers, teachers, work colleagues, employers, or employees.

There is a real danger middle children (and everyone around them for that matter) are taking on all these judgements, and absorbing the deficits and projections from others. This not only happens throughout their early formative years, but middle children can also carry this role throughout their adolescence and into adulthood, potentially continuing these effects whilst discharging their own parenting responsibilities. That's not very useful at all for middle children, the parents of middle children, nor their own children.

This is something that really needs addressing. I will do my bit in this chapter, but others need to follow with more insight, research and theories please.

We need to come to terms with what being a middle child is all about. We can be more positive. With information, awareness, and understanding we can all learn to make the best of our experiences of, and interactions with, middle children. There are rays of hope, there are many positive attributes we can ascribe. Some of them thankfully borne out in formal and proper research, and the occasional (interesting but less reliable) surveys and magazine articles. It is about time we considerately edited the narrative and rewrote the experience and ambition of middle children. It's time to turn the tables, recognise the challenges of being in the middle and review and celebrate the qualities and skills that can be developed within it. There is much good to find, and we can use it all to create a killer CV for the life and work of all middle children.

Healthy curiosity.

If you've been born, and have siblings, or not (I guess that covers all of us), I would bet there's going to be a bit of you that has been curious about birth order or family hierarchies. If you are a sibling, or parent of a middle child, you might have spent more than a few moments thinking about it. If you are a middle child yourself, you have most likely given it some serious thought.

It is quite common to overhear people asking each other if they were the oldest, the youngest, or an only child. I caught myself asking the butcher this morning; after casually mentioning I was editing this chapter today. Turns out he has a middle brother (he eye-rolled at the thought), and he is the oldest (as I suspected). Most of these enquiries are like petrol to our social curiosity, inform our five cent psychiatry, and reinforce our half-baked theories. They open the door to uninvited judgements, strengthen stereotyping, and gift-wrap insults with humour.

As we have already learned, there is also much wisdom and conversation to be found in a barbers' shop. A friend who had just read a draft of this book went for a trim the next day. The barber mentioned his older brother. *"Just the one brother?"* my friend asked, clearly his curiosity had been sparked. *"I have a sister too"* he replied, *"she's younger"*. *"So, you're the middle child?"* he nudged. *"Yep!"* quickly came the reply accompanied by a massive eye roll. *"Why don't you tell me about that?"* my friend invited. What followed was, according to my friend, was everything in this chapter, the older brother having the advantages and the accolades, the younger sister being fussed over, and the middle battling through *"hard graft"* to achieve their place in life. He felt he was the sibling with the most responsibility, with the greatest need to adapt and learn to create his own identity and pathway, with greater independence and distance from the family. Not statistically relevant research I grant you, but it tickled me to think the book was being talked about in a barbers' shop even before it was in print.

Like me and my butcher, you may be the first to arrive on the family scene, or you may be the last (thereafter and always known as the 'baby').

These family positions seem to have reputations and roles in common folklore and that is where I think lots of uncertainty and unhelpful thinking begins.

If you are a middle child, you will be conversant with the conditions associated with being in the middle. You may be all too familiar with the notion of fitting in and the dynamics of your place in the family. This, after all, will have most likely been a daily consideration, whilst watching all the comings and goings of family life around you. You will probably have found lots of resonance with the chapters on middle class and middle age. But like those other middles, and as I have said, being a middle child is a situation defined by what you are not. You are somewhere in between, left to deal with the melee of life sandwiched between your older and younger siblings. And that can be a busy space.

Because I haven't been a middle child, I wanted to add to what I had read and speak with some myself. Whilst I am friends with some, and work with others, I needed to ask some questions. This wasn't a formal research project, instead it was more of an organic journey over months and years. The middle-borns I have interviewed for this book ALL seemed surprised I was devoting my time to their lived experience and the general subject at all. So unused to attention as they were. That was my first finding. More of that later, but let's think about some of the theories first.

All in order.

Some people have come to think birth order has a significant effect on personality development. I like Alfred Alder's 1964 theory. He was a contemporary and student of Freud and founded the school of individual counselling and psychotherapy.

Helen Koch was an American developmental psychologist who developed nursery school teacher training programmes during the 1940s. She researched sibling order and also found birth order shaped personality, and that human development was also influenced by the gender and age differences between siblings. Koch found firstborns often received more parental attention and resources, which could lead to higher achievement and leadership qualities. In contrast, later-born children might develop alternative strategies to gain attention from their parents and others, and as such may be more sociable and cooperative. Koch suggested both parents and society had different expectations for children based on their birth order. Which for me is why people are quick to ask so they can reach and reinforce their definitions, just like they do with age. It makes me think we should never reveal our family position when asked and plead the fifth instead. For example, firstborns might be expected to be more responsible and mature – which places a great deal of more responsibility and maturity on the subject, whilst younger siblings might be seen as more carefree and rebellious – and have a more interesting time of it as a result.

Alder thought the oldest and the youngest children had more clearly defined roles within the family structure and in the parent-to-child interactions. I feel this is in line with what people generally think in society. The middle, and this is our particular interest of course, apparently had trouble fitting in. There was no clearly defined role for a child born (or placed) in the middle. As such, they ran the risk of receiving a deficit of attention and lower expectations of their future achievements. As a result, Alder thought middle children's hopes and behaviours were tempered, which made them more balanced individuals, with mostly quieter personalities. He did though think middleborns were the most successful of all. That all sounds relatively positive, something potentially to the annoyance of the older child at least. But the key question for me is: does freedom and a reduced amount of parental scrutiny and expectations result in positive outcomes for middles? Because some of us might immediately think a paucity of parenting attention would be a bad thing. Especially these days when modern helicopter-style parenting is following a high attention, high investment and interference model, by that I mean there is lots of control and attention giving and direct supervision at the expense of freedom, risk, and invaluable character forming alone time.

The youngest child is commonly thought to be the 'baby' of the family, seemingly finding it difficult to rise above their other siblings, no matter how old they were in childhood and in later adulthood. If you were the baby of the family, you always were (and are) the baby of the family. The associated behaviours and attributes of the youngest born can be tricky to shake off. The youngest child can attract elevated levels of care from one or both parents, whether that was needed or wanted, or not. An approach sometimes also mirrored by the older siblings. I have an instinct this is connected to some parent(s) 'hanging on' as long as possible to the direct and dependent parenting role. A manifestation of the attempts to make one last 'best attempt' at the rearing of offspring, or to delay the fledging of their last offspring, so not to expose what remains (such as their middle age).

The first child.

There are more first children than there are seconds and other children. It is often said (including by my own mother) parents make all their mistakes with the first, as they learn parenting 'on-the-job'. Did I mention I am a first child?

Children don't come with a manual and first-time child rearing is a blend of guesswork, reading, Googling (these days), and welcome and unwanted advice from friends and family. Even if there was a definitive manual, I don't think people would read it anyway. We ought to be cautiously aware of so-called parenting experts, their books weigh far too heavily on the shelves.

Parents, in the main, seek to invest their care and attention to support their children to achieve their best potential. And as they do so, their children keenly observe the nuances and differences in these behaviours. Children start to understand how they are treated, compared to others. And order, fairness, and justice are constant themes in sibling rivalry and personality development for children. Just like the workforce scrutinises their leaders and managers, they say 'I wouldn't have done it like that', 'if it was me I would have decided differently'. In the workplace, colleagues consider how others in the 'work family' are treated, who is the favourite, and how attention and rewards are distributed.

The social attitudes and working-class traditions of the pre-internet 1960s were a significant factor in my own upbringing. There were no computers. There was no Google. There were no parenting books on the shelves of our household, not even Dr Spock's best-selling Baby and Childcare published in 1946 (the year my own mother was born). Therefore, inter-generational approaches were the most likely option used. Which was sort of in line with Spock's philosophy that mothers *"know more than you think you do"*. The solution to teething? *"Pop some brandy in his milk"*, said my grandma. Misbehaving? *"A smack won't do any harm"*, said the whole of society it seemed. *"Spare the rod, spoil the child"*, said The Bible (well I paraphrase, but that is the gist). And so on. And so on.

Times move on, thankfully. Social attitudes and ideas about health, parenting and childcare change like the seasons. Sometimes appropriately, sometimes not. There appears to be less reliance upon intergenerational advice now we have 'Auntie Google', there we can find the benefit of wisdom, culture and traditions from a truly global family. That is both advantageous and a complete and utter headache.

Alder likened first-borns to alpha males in primate societies particularly in their coveting of power and status. He found a tendency to be dominant, aggressive, ambitious, jealous, and conservative. Quite the cocktail. It is a role either adopted by the child or a result of the expectations foisted upon them by their first-time parents, or the impact of having to share the spotlight with other offspring as and when they arrived on the scene. Alder found the older child to be more authoritarian — due to what he thought were those high expectations their parents placed upon them. He believed the first born held all the hopes and expectations of parenthood and gain the meticulous attention of their new parents. This was said by Alder to build a role of responsibility and leadership.

Society generally agrees with Alder I think. And if a family stops at the first, for whatever reason, then they have an 'only child', and they too receive all sorts of other judgements. Common opinions about only children include a mix of stereotypes and more nuanced views. Only children are sometimes perceived as being more selfish and spoiled due to receiving the undivided attention of their parents. There's a common belief only children might feel lonely without having the benefit of siblings to play and interact with. Some think only children can be overbearing or inflexible because they were not used to sharing or compromising with siblings in their formative years. That hasn't been my experience of only children I know. For balance, people also ascribe characteristics of high achievement and motivation, and this has been borne out in research. As has their maturity, independence, and social skills being developed earlier, as they often interact more with adults than peers. Other research has found these traits are not universally true.

This is not something I want to dwell on here. I am sure there is more for you to read out there on that subject.

Second time lucky.

The second child becomes the new baby of the brood. Second or later children are generally considered to benefit from a little less attention from parents who learned their lessons with the first child. The key advantage being less anxious childcare approaches, lower expectations, and the promotion of greater freedoms. That's the view I have, from my perspective of being the first born and the brother of a second son. As the older child of two, I very much thought things were easier for my younger brother with almost everything. I suspect he would disagree that was the case, if I dared ask. I haven't.

Third time's a charm.

But then, what happens if there is a third child or more children? Well, then you have a middle child or children. Congratulations! And everything changes again. For everyone. The first child is still the first, but attention must now also be shared with the second and the third.

And the middle child is no longer the baby, nor the focus of the new attention from parents. And that is when some even more interesting family and sibling dynamics start to happen. Parents start to twig they have help in the form of the child in the middle. Someone who will learn from the oldest, perhaps nurture the youngest, and will be able to support sibling relationships from now on – giving the parents some well-earned time respite.

Beyond the middle child to parent(s) dynamic, there is a significant influence from siblings. Middle children benefit from the unique opportunity to learn all sorts of useful (and useless things) from their older brother or sister – including many lessons parents don't always tell you. The really useful things in a child's life like where to go, who to hang out with, what to say, how to get away with misdemeanours etc. And in turn, the middle child can themselves educate and nurture their own little protégé in the form of their younger sibling(s).

Middle children spend their formative years looking up to the older, and looking down at their younger siblings, no doubt feeling inferior or superior in equal measure. Just like in that social class sketch. They drink in observations and learn from them. The timing of arrivals (the age gaps) and the gender differences will also have significant effects on their experience and development. All offering different flavours to various experiences. Alder said that *"in the drama of sibling competition, birth order and gender appear to be the most important players in the choice of sibling strategies… like a game of chess, coordinating tactics in age and gender sensitive ways"*. The result being the personality that is developed.

Journalist Katrin Schumann and psychologist Catherine Salmon thought the skills of relating well to older and younger people went someway to explaining why middle's work relationships and teamwork were potentially so strong. I guess there's something there about an observed empathy. One that has been polished through keen observation and understanding others' needs. Putting those first before your own. As someone who has occupied the margins, I know there is plenty of time and opportunity to drink in the actions, needs, neuroses, and postures of those in the immediate vicinity. Through such observations one can hone

"...in the drama of sibling competition, birth order and gender appear to be the most important players in the choice of sibling strategies... like a game of chess, coordinating tactics in age and gender sensitive ways."

———○———

Alfred Alder

razor sharp insight, social awareness, skills and techniques and a killer (but defensive) wit. All great life and work skills. Essential for careers in education, social care, and psychotherapy I would say. This time spent and the skills acquired ought to be accredited by someone.

Twins or multiple births.

Even a matter of minutes can be a factor in birth order and family hierarchies. It would be easy to think that such close birth order wouldn't be a consideration. But it really does connect with Adler's theories of psychological order rather than numerical order. With twins and triplets, the decisions and the roles assumed are formed through finely subtle shades of meaning or expression. You will find later that the thinking of the twin I spoke with for this book absolutely resonated with birth order theory.

Parenting in mind.

Clearly, the relationship we have with siblings is one factor that profoundly influences our development. Another influence is our connection and attachment (or not) with our parent(s). Whatever position you occupy in the sibling running order, you will most likely have an opinion on how you've been parented. All this conjecture might occupy a little bit, a medium sized bit, or a big bit of you. For some, it is mild curiosity or an amusement, for others it can be an all-consuming and distracting diversion, a disabling long-term blockage.

As an early years practitioner and childcare strategist, I appreciate how positive attachments and learning experiences are essential in forming a young child's brain and in supporting their personal, social and emotional development. As a psychotherapist, I have also been trained to deeply understand that these early experiences and attachments create the blueprint for our future behaviours, life patterns, and choices. And they really do. As a counsellor, making sense of a client's early years unlocks their understanding and releases the potential for reconciliation and resolution of the past to create positive choices moving forward.

It is a very good thing indeed to look in detail at our early experiences and how they have shaped our childhood development, and our adult lives and relationships at home and at work that follow. It is essential that we let go of what was destructive and unhelpful so we can replace it with constructive conscious alternatives. We need to understand what made us, and then remake ourselves.

Nest life.

All of this makes me think of the competing demands of fledgling birds in a nest. Three chicks, quietly awaiting a feed from their exhausted parents. When they regularly arrive with beaks bursting with a bounty of bugs, their expectant offspring chirp and squeak with beaks wide open to secure their fair share – or not as it happens. The first to hatch is bold and strong and assertive. It is physically bigger and more powerful than the other two. The advantage of time, even if they are only a few short hours is played out. There is no problem getting the worm for the oldest hatchling. The youngest, smallest, weaker, and perhaps more vulnerable chick has some competition. Their only hope is to grab the attention of the parent birds. They may notice the need to barge past the demanding first born, and ensure the little one gets nourished. They may not, and the last to hatch might actually fail to gain the nourishment they need. All this happens in front of the middle chick, who notices all that is going on. They may not always get their fair share of the grubs on offer either. That can shape and influence how they behave next time. They may need to change their strategy so they get the attention, and the worms they need, to survive and thrive.

In the family home, this same scenario can play out around the breakfast table, at family parties, on holidays, in the car, in the supermarket, basically anywhere where the whole family unit is together and when there are competing needs and demands. Not just where food is concerned. But that can be a common theme in sibling rivalry. Like who gets the first (or last) slice of pie, how many strawberries are in everyone's bowls, how much fizzy pop has been drunk, and the amount spent on birthday gifts. The themes of fairness and balance will no doubt play out powerfully throughout many of these complex family transactions. These events will form and shape the childhoods and adulthoods to follow. Just think about sibling rivalries at the reading of their late parents' wills, if you would like a concrete example. The stuff of drama.

Pecking order.

Where one settles in a nest or elsewhere, is clearly an important consideration for most of us. Where one fits-in seems such a constant preoccupation of any creature, humans included. Think about when you get an invite to a party or not, where you land on a wedding seating plan, your position in a queue, your role in a team, your location in the office, your closeness to your parents – the list is endless. We are obsessed with positioning and status. I say more about that in the chapter on middle place.

When I kept chickens, I learned very quickly that the hen house needed a slanted perch. It was urgently pointed out to me when I bought my first hen house. This is so the dominant bird, the one at the top of the pecking order, the one that mercilessly pecks away at the others to secure the top position, could roost at the highest level, leaving the others to work out their lower down positions after that. A level perch is the recipe for disaster, feathers will literally and inevitably fly. There's no flat structure in a chicken coop. There's always a hierarchy. Always a cock of the walk.

Amongst all this busyness, being the middle child can offer the sanctuary of the shadows. That space between the pressure and spotlight the oldest child attracts, and the forgiving soft-focus the youngest born benefits from. This offers the middle child a quiet space to process and learn and decide their own path of discovery. This is an advantage.

Disappointingly, all the valuable, positive and informed observations of Salmon and Schumann were once reported in a magazine feature entitled '5 reasons why being the middle child is actually the best'. Our target, our aim, needs to shed the unjustifiable negatives about the middle, and to set out and promote all the positives, without falling into the trap of super competitive jostling and status positioning. We don't need to be asserting that the middle child is the best. Surely, being good enough, is good enough?

It's perfectly acceptable to not be the best. Being good enough is where we find peace and solace. Like in parenting. The 'good enough' parent is a concept created from the work of English paediatrician and psychoanalyst D.W. Winnicott. He championed the concept of the *"ordinary good mother...the devoted mother"*. Not a super-mum, not the best, not the worst, but satisfactorily and functionally somewhere in between, in the middle of that. This was an assertion against what Winnicott saw was a rising tide of professional judgement and a growing involvement and concern of the state during the twentieth century to get involved in the household and the business of rearing offspring. Some things have not changed.

Let's value the middle without detriment to others shall we? That way we can all get on with each other better together in the middle.

Like a team always changes when someone joins or leaves, so birth order or sibling position is affected when children unfortunately die, or more happily, are born into a family. They change unpredictably when families become blended as relationships end and new ones begin, and new lineages of children come together. Alder used the term 'dethronement' when describing the experience of when a new sibling arrives on the scene. I like that idea. The existing children feel nudged out of their seat of power. And with highly dynamic family units and structures, there is much change and pushing for position to be negotiated.

In royal circles, births are literally all about dethronement and lines of power and succession. Monarchs and courtiers can become obsessed with securing their line of succession – people have died. It affects business too. A queue forms of likely natural or default successors to the power of the throne or the chairpersonship of the board. Who is next, then next and so on? Each birth or new recruit into the boardroom, literally dethrones a close relative or colleague. Popping them down a gold encrusted, bejewelled or bonus-laden peg or two. An event that may promote relief or envy in equal measure. It is the stuff that fuels scheming and plotting, revenge and treason. As history tells us, heads can roll, people can be 'disappeared', banished, deported, relocated, married off, paid off, or imprisoned so the desired political, religious or corporate power is secured.

Unhelpful thoughts.

We need to think about the awful term: 'middle child syndrome'. Like 'midlife crisis' I really don't think there is space in our lives for such an unnecessary term. The syndrome is the common view that the ascribed qualities of middle children somehow merit a diagnosis as they 'suffer' from the consequences of their place, choices, and patterns of inadequate or reinforcing parental approaches.

Naturally, I aim to focus on the positives and progressive ways forward. I wondered if middle child syndrome was really a thing. I mean, do we need a syndrome, any syndrome, in the first place? A syndrome is a group of symptoms, and symptoms are always undesirable and typically indicate a disease, problem, or something that society has an inexplicable difficulty with adjusting to. That is way off beat for me. It places the burden of blame on the child or adult, rather than requiring society to take its own responsibility. I am not a fan of medical models, labels, stereotypes and generalist trends either. I am in an eternal pursuit of socially aware alternatives.

Middle child syndrome should be a designated a myth. It is unnecessary and unhelpful and unfounded. That doesn't make it any less potent or harmful though. Myths still have traction. And this one has already seeped into social thinking. We need to search, alt, and delete it.

There are new insights to learn, and they need to offer us all helpful understanding to support middle children, their siblings, parents, friends and/or work colleagues. We can do that without creating a problem or syndrome. That is too conventional, too clinical, for me. Conventional thinking isn't useful for now and what comes next. We need to let go of it. The middle child needs to be looked at in a much more positive and inclusive way. What we all need, is something that offers us all essential awareness and guidance, and things for people to rethink. To help them achieve happiness in life and work.

Being positive about the middle child.

Schumann and Salmon, in a great mix of research and real-life stories, sought to redress the perceived imbalance and developed a philosophy, one that I like. Their book: The Secret Power of Middle Children (2011) reflected on our tendency to overlook or negatively consider the middle child. They aimed to release the mysteries that had evaded the rest of us so far, and shine a light on the positive alternatives.

They believed middle children were often overlooked, and they turn this into an opportunity for strength and self-development. They said it was the presence of less pressure (than their siblings) that helped generate greater independence and self-assurance. Their research showed that *"as middles mature they gain self-confidence — this likely has to do with them recognizing and valuing innate strengths, and downplaying perceived weaknesses"*.

They also thought that by being caught in the middle of the dynamic between older and younger siblings, they had a unique position that offered an older role model and a younger mentee. In being in this space, they honed their skills for negotiation, diplomacy, listening, and peace-keeping. All skills I like in the workplace in my team, I must say. Maybe I could start asking candidates this. Although I am not sure HR would stand for that.

Nature and nurture.

Everyone is an individual and anything that identifies tendencies or observations should be taken with a healthy dose of salt, a little like horoscopes. They may offer us some trends and generalisations that

"...as middles mature they gain self-confidence — this likely has to do with them recognizing and valuing innate strengths, and downplaying perceived weaknesses."

Schumann
and Salmon

can be useful in promoting self-reflection – but they aren't something to gamble your working class wages or your middle class salary on. They do tell us something, as Sheldon in the US TV sit-com The Big Bang Theory acerbically observed in the first episode, if you believe in astrology *"it tells us that you participate in the mass cultural delusion that the sun's apparent position relative to arbitrarily defined constellations at the time of your birth somehow affects your personality"*. Love him.

I more-or-less received the same parenting as my younger brother and enjoyed the same social and economic conditions. Excepting that I was the first born and he was the second. We went to the same secondary school. But we have grown into two very different people. It is our own personal reaction and relationship to such external factors and experiences that contributed to the shaping of our personalities and life choices.

I have had the benefit of lots of people in my life and at work. Many of them middles or parents of middle children. In early years, I have worked with many families and children, and that has taught me a lot. At work, I have learned much about different people in teams and organisations. And in psychotherapy I have noticed how clients relate to their siblings, and often struggle with that, and how they are concerned with their relationship with their parents. All this forms much of the foundation of my thinking. So, to add to my learning and reflections, and those of others, collected along the way, I set out to interview people with direct experience of being a middle child.

Talking with middles.

It was always going to be important I talk with others about their experiences of being a middle child. I wanted to hear from those around me who had lived as a middle child or parented them as well.

I embarked on a journey of speaking with various people I knew to be middles. They were friends and colleagues who have revealed their middle status as they learned about the book, and/or friends of friends kind enough to make an introduction. I have met with young people who were middle children, I have met with adults who reflected on their middle childhood now and then, parents of middle children, even middle children who are now parents of middle children. Some of this was planned and deliberate, the rest of it was circumstantial, accidental on occasion.

I shared with them my personal and professional observations and the outcome of reading and research, listening intently to their lived experiences and seeking to connect all that together to make sense of it all. What was extraordinary was all their responses. It was so common to hear interviewees share feelings of nerves or anxiety derived from not liking the focus or attention. Because focus and attention seemed so alien to them. Some said, well that will be a short chapter, *"ha ha!"* There was also a sense of fear that their contributions wouldn't be useful or interesting enough. *What is there to say?*, they would ask. Then there were the people pleasers, completely focused on ensuring they were giving me exactly what I needed. It was striking that all those being interviewed kept asking if their input was useful at all. It was like their thoughts and feelings were somehow of less worth than those of others. They were surprised to be asked. *Why the interest?* There was also a strong sense and need to please people (me) – to make the lives of others the happiest they could be. I don't think you would get that with a first born (theorists may disagree given the stronger attachment to adult attention perhaps), or a last born I thought. I am aware I am making a sweeping generalisation.

I bumped into a middle child friend of mine on the street one day. I told her about writing this book. I talked about all the other chapters first, and then said there was one on the middle child. Her face had already started to change. She could see that one coming. Her eyes sparkled and she shared her instant reaction – *"oh yes"*. Well, that unsurprisingly sparked my interest. I'd been hopeful she would sit down with me and tell me her story. She detonated a plentiful sequence of words at me. Things like mediation, negotiation and conflict resolution, she talked about being caught in the middle of all the drama. She laughed whilst she rolled her eyes (a common reaction I found when talking with middle children). There was too much to take in, I needed my notebook, it wasn't to hand, but I certainly opened my diary and booked in an interview. I sought out other friends, family, and colleagues. It wasn't a random or a scientific sample. Merely a social network with shared experiences. Sometimes 'interviews' lasted a few brief moments when doing something else. Sometimes they lasted all afternoon. Sometimes they took the form of observations and things overheard.

I spoke with a twin who was only minutes younger than his brother, a time difference that created his position and clear feelings as the middle child. The time and age difference was always there. He talked about how twin friends hadn't been told the time difference, or who was the oldest or the youngest in an attempt to avoid such hierarchical posturing.

A middle child, now in middle age very quickly shared she had adopted a position of responsibility early on. She wanted to be the 'good one', easily accepting and not fighting what was decided. Accepting a no was a no. In times of family conflict, it was better to keep one's head down and wait for things to die down. And wait until the show was over. It was not her role to push the boundaries, merely to live within them. Such a pattern of behaviour continued into adulthood with a large circle of 'friends for life', a propensity to care for people, and a busy social life. *"Just getting on with life and work"*, she said, *"you have no choice"*.

A middle child who had become the mother of three, and a mum of a middle child, said she did not want to treat her middle like he was a middle. She wanted her child to be treated equally and not be child carer for their younger sibling.

They connected with the idea of looking up to the older sibling as a role model and caring for the younger one. They said a middle child's life can be busy and loud and full of interactions, with lots of children, friends in and out, in a larger family.

Many had overheard the thoughts of others in the general public, of media pundits, about 'middle child syndrome' – a stream of negativity. *"Rarely have I heard anything positive about being the middle child"*. This is such a shame to hear it directly confirmed. There is something equally as special about the middle child as the older or the younger ones. *"The thing about the middle is it all seems so mediocre"*. That comment hit the nail right on the head.

What themes do they share?

-Being overlooked. Yes, there were feelings about being forgotten, and connecting with the concept of the effects of not being the first 'special' child, neither being the cutest or most vulnerable youngest one. What was striking was that actually very little time had been spent properly and carefully thinking about their own social experiences of being the middle child. Most likely a result of putting everyone else's needs first, or the parenting spotlights being trained upon the others, and the paucity of useful content out there to help value it and make sense of it.

-Untitled. Middles would often tell me that as a middle child, you have no title, you're not the oldest or the youngest. And that it felt attention was directed at the first and last borns. You're not at the top and you're not at the bottom – just like Robin the Frog.

-Being that bridge. And what was learned through their lived experiences? The ability to understand both sides of any of the frequent arguments. *"I can always see the grey between the black and the white. I say things like, well what about seeing things differently?"* when getting embroiled in family 'debates'. I was struck by the role the middle child was circumstantially required to adopt when it came to sorting out a family's small, medium, and larger problems. And I truly feel sorry for that. It seems like a life sentence – a trap. And it may not be limited to being in between siblings, and it can become the space in between one's parents, friends and work colleagues as well. Being that bridge.

-Watching. I recognised the learned skills in being able to step back from the distractions of what is actually happening and read the bass line. Abilities honed by exceptional observation and listening skills. Instead focusing on the core business at hand – and what the reality is and what needs to happen next. That's not about being dispassionate or unemotional, but it is about anticipation and resolution. Adopting the middle ground. There was also a sense of not expressing their own opinion in such matters so it isn't divisive or gets in the way. A childhood of noticing the signs, can create expert behaviour readers in adulthood. They become that invaluable person who can spot the signs of distress and upset in others far earlier than others notice. They are expert behaviour readers. Middles said to me *"I now generally try to avoid conflict. I feel more confident in smaller groups, and rarely if ever am I looking for a wider audience. I don't shirk from tackling difficult issues, or suggesting solutions and I have a strong moral compass. But I don't always want to be in the thick of it."* Even though many of them felt a strong pull from the family to bring them into the mediator role. In childhood, as we know, roles and behaviours are quickly established and such habits can be hard to break.

-State of independence. There was a sense of a grown independence away from the family. Closeness with their families remained, but it was probably best described as self-sufficiency. Parents of grown-up middles might feel less close to, or dependent upon them. Indeed, Salmon and Schumann argued middle children received less financial and emotional support from their parents, yet become remarkably successful and innovative adults. They observed middles can be stubbornly independent as teens. I certainly found resonance with this. Certainly some, not all, of those I spoke with felt they had less financial and emotional support than their siblings. That's a difficult subject for any family to discuss without emotional tension. Yes, they could be stubbornly independent as teenagers. As adults, they perhaps were less used to sharing problems with parents or the wider family – at least automatically or at first. Perhaps as a result of them forming their own network of friends to go to instead. They often tended to mostly deal with difficulties themselves or with their constructed support networks, but that did not exclude their partners and their families. The birth order dynamics can be altered when children leave, to university for example, or move out permanently. This can be unsettling for the remaining child or children. And whilst the hierarchy remains, the geography can shift the dynamics of family status and behaviours.

Especially if the middle child becomes absent. There is no one left to be the practical organiser and facilitator, the conflict diffuser.

-Reflections. The interviews showed me how many of the lived experiences correlated with the theory I had read. It was fascinating to me, when listening to people talking about their past experiences of being middle children (or parenting one), also observing or hearing about their current experiences as adults. It seemed to me that much of the birth order parenting approaches in childhood had carried on throughout their adulthood. Any experience of being a middle child was of course also influenced by gender, age differences and familial arrangements. All of our experiences are unique, as are our families. As I said, commonly my interviewees would be surprised I was asking them about these things, and they were totally convinced they wouldn't be of much use or interest to me. In reality, the opposite was the case. I would ask interviewees if they felt successful. However, they measured it. This was puzzling to many, as they often weren't thinking about themselves in that way. Some were in long-term relationships, had a strong group of older and younger friends, enjoyed great cross generational social skills, held interesting jobs, and had wonderful customer service skills. Sounded pretty good to me, but not necessarily to them.

Building on the capacity for middle children's roles to continue within the family construct throughout the lifetime of the family, in their adult relationships, and at work, I also noticed how middle children looked elsewhere to fill the perceived or actual shortfall of their family's relational sustenance. They may attach to personal relationships earlier, quicker and stronger. They may seek to grow their own family unit, or construct a thriving social network of meaningful friendships often with older and younger friends – not surprising given the social skills they have developed living with older and younger siblings, and negotiating with parents. In these spaces they can be themselves, not just someone defined by what they are not, to become more than the filling in the 'sibling sandwich'. They can construct their own family unit and their position within it. To end this section on another positive, one said: *"I would say the best bits are the opportunity to receive a more relaxed parenting experience than your brothers or sisters. You potentially are given space for yourself, and you don't have as much pressure as the others".*

Finally, I asked for advice from middles to other middles: There was a strong theme of making the most of the experience and to do your best. Some of that involved focusing on the advantages, being positive, and keeping your head down, safe in the knowledge your learned social skills will forge lifelong friendships. There was also a reminder the lack of scrutiny means you have a great deal of freedom to get away with things.

At the end of interviews and when given the opportunity to read the first draft of the chapter, and or the extracts that included their content, it was gratifying and fascinating to hear interviewees say it had put a smile on their face. They welcomed the dedicated time (which they had never done before) reading and thinking about the middle and finding out about the different theories and thoughts out there. There was an appreciation of the skills developed through the experience of being a middle child and *"the unique perspective that being in the middle has given me which I've never previously considered".*

Owning it.

The middle child's experience may not always need to be passive or pre-determined. The middle child may find a great need to directly compete with their brothers and sisters not only for food, but for attention, and recognition. They may not ever feel they are the favourite of the brood. They will certainly feel the effects of being in a group or a team though. If it isn't managed well, then this can lead to deliberate choices to reject, rebel or choose alternative lifestyles or values – so they garner a little more attention or attract some of the much-needed limelight. You don't need me to list the ways in which children and young people can rebel for attention. These choices need not be damaging or negative – they could be innovative, creative, inventive – funny even. Their efforts resulting in bright new independent futures. Alder said that siblings make efforts to be different in unoccupied niches, due to their Darwinian interests, as diversity diminishes the competition for finite resources.

The middle child needs to reconcile their upbringing and use the experience for a well-rounded adulthood at a time that suits them. As we have learned, middle children are frequently thought to be better at conflict resolution and peace making. But if these skills aren't honed well, then their desire for attention may generate unhealthy or unsafe behaviours. They may hold on to a deep sense of inadequacy or inferiority, which could fuel low self-worth.

There is a risk unresolved and unconsidered childhood reverberations lay dormant and buried until middle life at which point it may need more serious attention. This book is all about the positive, so if and when that occurs, it requires positive action to resolve it. There is useful content in the middle age chapter on that.

Deciding your path.

Middles may shine brighter than everyone else, have developed well practiced sharing and listening skills. If I was a middle child, I might already be feeling especially tired of this expectation. Many may reject the idea of being consigned to the negotiator role – wanting more from their life than being the Secretary General of the UN, or a marriage counsellor, or such like. Because let's face it – this is pretty much the middle position and is only serving to extend the middle position they have always adopted. Middle children may prefer instead to take more risks, be a leader and/or be more entrepreneurial. Their understanding of the life of the 'second best' may drive a desire to settle the world's injustices and enter into a humanitarian or campaigning career. Plenty of famous people, presidents and highly successful businesspeople are middle children. Some offer good role models, others less so. Schumann pointed out in a story for the Daily Mail, that 52% of all US Presidents (since 1787) were middle children. But I wonder whether that was more a consequence of middle-class families predilection to have larger families, of typically three or more children, or the fashion or social requirement to counter the effects of child mortality through the eighteenth and nineteenth centuries. Or maybe they were seeking an unconventional career that just so happened result in being president. And I noticed that some people described as middle-borns in the past, weren't actually, because the birth of female siblings wasn't taken into consideration back then. That may or may not surprise you. It shocked me.

What do parents need to know?

There is a fine balance to achieve in parenting, any parenting. Parents, and anyone working with children, want to support and stretch them, to help them feel safe and to open their opportunities. We aim to give them the confidence to believe in themselves, so they best pursue their lives and dreams ahead. I fully support that endeavour. But we must be realistic. There is nothing worse than over-promising and under-delivering in any aspect of life. By that I mean we could be wary of telling our children they can do anything, be anyone, go anywhere. This just isn't the case for so many of them.

Instead, we can help our children discover happiness, so they know who and what they are, and can use that knowledge to become happy with who they are, and what they will do now and later. They must not be distracted by unnecessary and unattainable fluff and fantasy. Nor should they feel implied pressure to become astronauts like that girl in the silver trousers at my storytelling event.

When it comes to bringing up a middle child, here is a little advice for parents. Some of it from me, some of it from books, and some of it from those I interviewed for this book. Remember I said beware of so-called parenting experts?

-Make, take, and give dedicated one-to-one time with your middle child. This is good for their emotional acknowledgment and could build their greater sense of being noticed in a lived experience that will often feel quite the opposite.

-Recognise when your child needs alone or apart time, not forcing onto them unwanted 'quality time' with you. And to allow for this to happen to build autonomy and responsibility. To let go.

-Work hard to notice and understand what strategies your middle child has developed, and is using, to attract your attention and of others around them. This may be positive (wanted) and negative (unwanted) behaviour. All responses to behaviour feel like a reward to a child.

-Middle children need to feel safely acknowledged when needing attention, and supported to develop the skills to receive attention in positive ways. This is the same for all children, but seems to be especially pertinent for the middle sibling.

-Focus on the positives and make sure your middle child knows you have noticed whatever they are doing that is desirable. You could ignore the unwanted in the main, choosing and prioritising what things need talking about, and what things you will let slide.

-Opportunities could be grasped to include your middle child in what is going on in the wider family. Adopt that mother or father bird role and ask yourself: does this chick need another worm? Filter out the noise of the oldest hatchling and put on hold for a moment the instinct to protect and nurture the little one. Bring the middle child into what is happening, what is being talked about, played, decided, discussed, or planned.

-For a middle child who is feeling they are stuck in the mediocre middle, parents can support their child's individualistic choices, sense of style, and self-worth.

-Help them to develop their own identity and stand out and proud beyond their birth-right invisibility into a confident and positive visibility instead.

Salmon and Schumann recommended parents move away from their obsession with attention giving, as a child's independence is a critical skill. Social interaction could be encouraged, along with a bit of parent to middle one-to-one time by making time and applying efforts to 'bring them to the table'. Parents could ask them questions (I would recommend doing that carefully and whilst everything else is happening, no one expects the Spanish Inquisition). The opportunity can arise when a child says something or displays a particular interest. Children could feel rewarded for being themselves. They also said pay lots (not too many) of compliments.

Last words.

Our early experiences including how we were parented and where we sat in the family hierarchy don't define the rest of our lives. *"Sibling strategies are not set in stone… evolution has equipped us all to be versatile strategists"* Sulloway p147. Yes, they have shaped us, but the skills and qualities we have developed then, and since, have given us the tools to steer our own direction and choices.

We can review, reconcile and reason. We must accept the fact that some children are born into the middle. There isn't a huge body of scientific or research proof of much of the theories relating to the middle child. We can all look beyond the myths and misunderstandings, or neglect, that middle children are subjected to, and to scrape under the surface of real lived experiences and reveal a deeper awareness and empathy. Let go of all that anti-middle child feelings and focus on the many advantages they will bring. Focus on their skills and qualities. I have shared many of my own observations, and like most social observations they are open to interpretation, speculation, the latest fashion, and counter-findings.

For middle children, the best advice is to relax and focus on all the brilliant and successful things they do. For those of us around, we could all be better in our interactions with middle children. Indeed, if you are the parent, carer or significant adult of any middle child, please play your part to help them develop a healthy and realistic relationship with everything middle. Middle children are all individuals, of course they are. But there seems to be evidence they are experts at personal and professional relationships – up and down. And have finely tuned understanding of people's needs. There is an opportunity to use this as a positive force. A middle child then might need help in developing their CVs. I would suggest a starting point could be:

- **amazing organiser**
- **a 'go to' mediator**
- **dependable**
- **calm**
- **practical**
- **fantastic listener**
- **logical**
- **loyal**
- **able to get on with all sorts of people**
- **perceptive to the point they anticipate people's needs and emotions earlier than anyone else around.**

I shall give the final word on the matter to Schumann: *"When they realise how many useful skills they've developed as a result of being in the middle, they are empowered in ways that positively influence their lives".*
I cannot put it better myself.

—o—

The middle at work

"I've been promoted to middle management. I never thought I'd sink so low."

───o───

**Tim Gould,
racing cyclist.**

Organisations always have a structure, whether you like it or not. Their basic and most positive aim is to help organise things and set out clear lines of accountability. Unfortunately, structures can also get in the way, and you guessed it, they can create all sorts of middles, as they form middle management tiers, and cause people to caught in the middle.

I meet lots of people who enjoy their time designing, redesigning and changing their organisational structures. Little do they know the effects of their toiling are relatively insignificant. By that I mean structures don't always offer positivity or helpful ideas, nor do they solve the identified problems they were supposed to solve. I believe they don't achieve half as much as their architects imagine they will. Instead, I think their time could be better dedicated to embedding values, creating culture, and fostering happiness and empowerment in the workforce and across the organisation. That is a people job, because it is people (not papers) that effect change, innovation, and impact – if only they dare move away from their desk and move around the shopfloor a little more.

Downward glances.

Why do I think this? Let me share a story. I was delivering a programme of government funded consultancy in English local authorities. This was after the Children Act in 2004, an extensive piece of legislation that followed in the wake of the Laming Inquiry into the death of Victoria Climbié. Like many reviews held after the tragedy of a child's death, the report found lots of missed opportunities and a catalogue of failures of those in parental, personal, and professional roles – often caused by a communications or process dysfunction in the middle. There is almost always a call for reform and restructure in the various reports that are commissioned. The difference then was Laming's ideas for reform were ambitious, bold, and far-reaching – and crucially, behavioural. My job involved visiting local councils to help them develop and enact their workforce reform plans, so they could fully meet the requirements of the Act. Early on, and even months into their implementation, I started to find many councils had only achieved rudimentary change in top management structural and reporting lines. They would start our meetings by proudly presenting their new structures, focused on how their internal management and division of responsibilities would change. That wasn't enough for me, I was strongly of the view they needed to be consulting, discussing, training, coproducing, and most importantly equipping and empowering their middle tier and frontline workforces. This was so they could all effect the change that was so desperately and urgently needed. The way in which top line management was functioning was much less important than these council leaders believed. And in some areas, a year on, nothing of any significance had changed at all. The buzz-words they used in reports might have been different, but certainly there was little evidence that behaviours and systems had been changed at all. Normally I would allow them to open the meeting and steer its direction. And so, a few weeks in I changed tack. I would start meetings by thanking the 4-6 senior managers for their time, reasserting the root purpose and the crucial nature of the task at hand, and the difference it could make. I would then say, *"before you take me through how you have restructured or propose to restructure. I would like the full story of how you have engaged and rebuilt relationships with the middle and frontline workforces in consultation, training, confidence building, communication, and change management. What have you found and what have they been telling you?"* Cue downward glances, widening or narrowing eyes, uncomfortable shifting in seats, and various changes in face colour. Point made, right there, right then. That's when I would see pennies dropping and changes about to begin. I guess my view is they are a starting point and something to build upon, and not rely upon.

Definitions, understanding, and structure are all important considerations, like with birth order and class. They must all work though, they must be positive, and they must help. They need managing and working within to ensure they deliver and don't hamper what they are aiming to achieve.

Hierarchies.

Unless you work alone, work always has hierarchies too. This is different to structure. Hierarchies can be deep, shallow, or somewhere in between. They can be defined or unspoken, rigid or changing, clear or unambiguous. Their characteristics can be either convenient or problematic to the business and those that work within it. Whilst different in type and nature, there is always someone at the top and someone at the bottom in a hierarchy. That means there will be something or someone in the middle as well.

If there are more than two people in a business or team, it is most likely there will be a middle as well. That is an important issue for everyone involved. Whether you are at the top looking down at the middle, at the bottom looking up at it, or if you are occupying that very space in between, or managing it, and getting a stiff neck from all that looking up and down.

Holding on and letting go.

Effective working relies on fulfilling all sorts of basic and essential business functions in our roles within the structure and the hierarchy. By that I mean we could be health and safety agents, people focused, sales hungry, finance concerned, decision-makers, and innovation creators – to list just a few goals. We need to be clear about our roles, and be able to achieve them, whilst adapting to the need to change.

I have observed or presided over enough staff or business restructures and reviews to know how powerfully attached some can be to their job roles. On the flip side, I have seen colleagues desperate to get rid of the unhelpful baggage of theirs. The restructure process can be a long and torturous one of negotiation and one that can be slow to realise the real change needed. I have even seen many reviews start before the previous one had concluded, applied, or evaluated. I've worked with clients who have been in the middle of such reshuffling for 10 years or more. All rather distracting, pointless, demotivating, and disempowering. I'd rather focus more attention and time on roles and contributions, and the impact and difference made in roles, than what it says on the virtual tin. I would rather we concentrated on delivery and enjoying our work and its effects. And I want people in the team and customers to be able to interact with each other equally and across all 'levels' of the people in the business hierarchy. You don't stand a chance of getting anywhere near these states of mind if the sword of Damocles is hanging above you in permanent threat of restructure or redundancy. It only serves to generate uncertainty, competition and self-preservation.

What does middle management mean?

The larger the organisation, the greater the likelihood there is a middle. Middle management, in basic terms, is the space between the bosses at the top and the workforce underneath, if you follow a traditional hierarchical structure that is. The flatter the structure the smaller and thinner the middle is, conversely, the deeper the structure then the fatter the middle becomes. In basic terms, the bosses set strategy, middle management do the planning and ensure it is implemented, the workers do the work. Sounds simple doesn't it?

It isn't that straight forward if you are working in that middle space. Being a middle manager can be described in a few ways. First, by the place one physically occupies in an organisation's structure. Second, where one sits in a communication chain. Third, where one is in relation to where the power lies. And fourth, if working across competing agendas, being mired in the middle of the mechanics, the message, the money, and the mission(s). Which, let's face it, in reality, is a lot of people working in a lot of organisations. These characteristics can give us our best days at work, and fuel the worst. Rarely an after-work rant to a partner or friend omits any of these four frankly infuriating factors.

I have certainly found myself in a middle management position before. I look back at that one with a reflective learning lens and a deep sense of relief the worst of it is all over. After quite a while, middle management is part of my life again. The standout memories for me were having to defend ill-thought-out spur-of-the-moment decisions by top management, that none of the staff team had been consulted upon, and didn't understand, or didn't want to support. This left me in the middle having to reconcile unrealistically large tasks with scant resources, whilst holding the feeling of being taken for granted, asked to inspire and motivate a team that felt the same. We were all let down by a lack of proper support, and overlooked when it mattered most.

We were soon noticed when there was more to do. They always found me when something needed doing. That doesn't sound great does it? On the plus side it felt like I was involved in much of the activity of the organisation. Until I didn't. Too often, it felt like I was nowhere near some of the top management activities I needed to be involved with, and was excluded from the thoughts and discussions being had by other staff. All of which would have better equipped me to communicate what everyone was thinking and needing. This resulted in me experiencing unreasonable levels of pressure and becoming stressed and depressed, in that order (it usually is). I wasn't faultless, I could have managed things better, said no instead of yes, and vice versa. But I was young, and I wasn't getting the line management support and coaching that such a role requires. I soon came to realise I wasn't the first, and wouldn't be the last to experience that in this place. For me, this was that familiar tale of fitting-in and not fitting-in. Of feeling in the middle of nowhere, in the margins – again. A similar experience of those born in the middle, of those seeking their place in the class structure, or resolving their age and stage of life. And like middle children, I learned a lot in that space to take forward into the rest of my career. Lessons to learn from, and some lessons not to be repeated.

Middle management gets bad press.

The nightmares associated with being a middle manager are commonly described as being caught in the 'in-between' and trying to keep everyone happy at all times. Just like the middle child and the middle class. This usually results in everyone feeling unhappy all of the time. Bosses want their decisions putting into action and they want to see results. The staff team is unhappy about what the bosses are asking for. Middle managers are left with the tricky task of working out how to pitch them, and to motivate the team to deliver them. They also have to report back to management about what is working and what is not.

In my own experience, the role of the middle manager is one that is frequently under-valued by those up the chain and those down it. It can feel like a thankless role, with many pitfalls and none of the freedoms of lower tiers, nor the perceived glamour and trappings of being the ones in charge. It can be a lonely place being the middle manager at the office Christmas party, walking the office corridors, walking through the car park at the end of the day, or sitting down for lunch – outnumbered by those above and below, and not quite being able to hear the muffled conversations happening around you. It needn't be like this.

One of the big problems is all the stuff written about middle management. It rarely sets the right tone in my view. This is another missed middle opportunity. Articles commonly couch the issue in negative terms of: crisis, survival, and distress. Just like how they describe middle age, things like: 'Identity crisis', 'Stuck in the middle', 'Survival guides', and 'Stay sane'. They all highlight the things that could be wrong or difficult:

-Struggling to fit in. Not being able to reconcile feelings of loneliness and unhappiness, and failing to settle on a role definition or purpose, whilst trying to appease everyone else.

-Lack of autonomy to make decisions. Or simply not being involved in the decision-making process, instead being expected to be the decision-enforcer – often with scant information to explain how and why decisions have been made.

-Being caught in between. In the middle of decision-makers and those most affected by them, i.e. the workforce, and soaking up all the associated dissatisfaction. Whilst at the same time feeling irritated and exasperated, powerless to do anything to change it. And teams soon getting frustrated with a lack of change and irritated with middle managers if they consider them to be part of the problem.

-Feeling 'set up'. Being asked to do the unpopular things the bosses don't want to, or dare not do themselves.

-Ups and downs. Middle managers can sometimes be ruthlessly, ambitiously, and impatiently on the way up to their future higher management roles. They are prepared to suffer some of these imperfections as their eyes are on greater prizes. Some may have reached their peak at this age and stage and are occupying the middle tier whilst coming to think they will not fulfil further ambitions. Something that is beautifully illustrated by this David Brent quote from The Office (UK version): *"Well, there's good news and bad news. The bad news is that Neil will be taking over both branches, and some of you will lose your jobs. Those of you who are kept on will have to relocate to Swindon, if you wanna stay. I know, gutting. On a more positive note, the good news is, I've been promoted, so... every cloud. You're still thinking about the bad news aren't you?"*

-Descending the career ladder. Some middle managers are on the demotivating, distressing, or comforting downward slide from top management – dropping down the pecking order as they get older and are dethroned by the shiny, new, and ambitious younger ones.

-Feeling under constant threat. An existential risk to the role, given the impact of technology and the trend for flatter structures and hierarchies in organisations. The role appears to business architects as being superfluous and bureaucratic. There is a risk of extinction, middle managers are often considered to be superfluous.

-Being miserable at work. In a useful example of the lived experiences of middle managers and the consequences of being stuck in the middle, in 2014 The Harvard Business Review reported the most miserable of 320,000 employees they interviewed were those 'stuck in the middle of everything'... receiving good, rather than brilliant or terrible performance ratings (Jacobs). There could be an argument that middle managers have higher levels of depression and anxiety. I certainly left my middle management position depressed, stressed, and exhausted. I rapidly recovered once I left it.

What happens as a result of all of this, is that everyone becomes really rather nervous and anxious, and even embarrassed by the middle at work. Just as class isn't always openly discussed in social circles so we don't appear discourteous or judgemental, middle management is often ignored at work for the very same reasons. A really good example follows.

I don't mean to be rude.

Sometimes we are just too polite. I was talking with a colleague who works in a large charitable organisation. I told her about writing this book. I'm always on the search for a case study, and this time I struck gold. She told me they had recently been organising a training conference for their middle managers. This was because they were the vital and skilled people in their structure who were responsible for leading customer and stakeholder facing work. An indispensable link in the organisational chain, I reckon. It transpired this vital link was described as middle managers within the privacy of the boardroom or top management meetings. The problem, they had come to realise, at the point of going public with the plan to support middle managers, was they didn't know what to call them. They didn't want to use the phrase 'middle managers'. Why might that be, I asked? It was thought too rude and disrespectful, I was told. And so, a rather clumsy and long alternative was applied instead. Are you ready for this? They went with 'staff who supervise or manage direct delivery of services'. Snappy wasn't it! I don't blame them, the issue is completely tricky. But apologetic management is really the worst kind of management isn't it? I mean it is like middle class householders apologising every time they ask their cleaners to vacuum the stairs. Of course this is related to the ideas of social class, this time the class structure within the business.

Business concerns.

Business isn't just concerned with structure, hierarchies, and power. Too much of the awful rhetoric surrounding business is about growth as well. I find it all too tiresome. I recoil every time I am invited to attend a networking event when the stated aim is to 'help us all connect so we can expand our businesses for growth'. Often, they simply appear to self-serve the self-promoting organisers of such things. Yawn. They seem to believe their own hype. I don't, so I rarely go anymore. What is their purpose I ask? Is it as basic as to sate the thirst to accumulate more money and profit, or is it to massage collective egos and build perceptions of power across the assembled gathering? Given the usual attendees are public relations (PR), media and marketing, pension advisers, financial advisers, and business coaches, I suspect all of that is the case. A community of coexistent services. Looking in from the margins, it seems like quite a small gene pool.

Rarely do the networking invites I receive focus on social value, or equality and diversity, or moral purpose. There's a huge gap in the market for that. Because if things were different, I believe a whole load of businesses who, like me, might actually engage and turn up – for all our benefit. Speaking as someone who does a fair bit of PR type work and business coaching that is. The fact is many people (not all) in business do seem focused only on growth, size, and scale. They buy the 'business-lit' on the airport bookstore shelves, that seeks to occupy lonely businesspeople on solitary work trips.

Mine is bigger than yours.

Businesses like buildings too. Business districts are full of huge phallic monoliths thrusting out into the sky to demonstrate the penetrative and potent power of the businessmen inside. Or to compensate for their lack of it. Now, I am not the first person to identify the link between city skyscrapers and penises, and I won't be the last. I'm not impressed by the trend to design such things, not the construction of increasingly ridiculous versions fashioned like cheese graters or walkie talkies. See the City of London, New York's financial district, Tokyo's Marunouchi, Sydney's central business district (CBD), and Dubai's Business Bay for illustrations of this point. I've been to them all and cricked my neck in shock and awe. Their architects have grown rich by pandering to businessmen's fragile egos by promising the biggest and tallest, most impressive, or novelty constructions.

The bigger the better. Few businesses, it seems to me, are setting out to have a medium sized head office are they? Or to create something that is an alternative to the obvious stiffy. That said, I watched with interest how the Google headquarters was developed in London's King's Cross. The first, wholly owned and designed Google building outside the US. A skyscraper on its side. 11 storeys high (modest in comparison), an extraordinary 1 million square feet. Room for 7,000 employees. Still big, still long, but resting, flaccid one might say. Sprawling across its estate. Very different to what we have come to expect. Will it be as potent I wonder? Or is it the ultimate symbol of power? Is the new 'thrusting into the sky' becoming a sprawling 'land grab' instead? The long term effects on hybrid working are as yet unknown.

The Ringelmann Effect

Then there are issues around the size of teams. Again, in my day job, I remember what happened to local council early years teams in England between the mid-1990s and the mid-2000s. Before then, I would visit councils and be lucky to find an early years officer at all. In one area, I remember they had two (one was part-time). They were great, knew everyone, did everything, and what they didn't know about early years and childcare wasn't worth knowing. They were battling in a world that still wasn't taking childcare and pre-school learning seriously, well a lot less seriously than it is taken now (and let me tell you there is still some way to go before that job is done). Fast forward to 2005, and the same council had over 100 people working in early years and childcare, plus a number of contracted organisations also beavering away. This was the result of seven years of escalating and generous funding from the government's first National Childcare Strategy. There was much good done in those times, and I wish things could at least swing back some way towards them. But I also found it the most frustrating thing. This team of 100 plus people was not great. I say team, they were not a team in a real sense. They didn't even know each other, and many people were in niche, unconnected and often competing or overlapping specialist roles. Their skill set was limited, not multi-disciplinary, and the team structure and hierarchy was clunky and dysfunctional. And they all needed to be told more than a thing or two about early years I can tell you. Things were slow and inefficient. Too much time was spent navigating the territory and organising the machine they had become. Leadership was well intended, strategic and informed, but the realities of the team's output meant that effectiveness was lost at the expense of overburdening those for whom the service was supposed to benefit. Simply put, there was too much unnecessary effort being applied in the middle of the team structure. It wasn't working. They had lost sight of their mission, of achieving outcomes, of making a positive impact. The energy was being spent feeding the system that was supposed to be supporting the sector, rather than for the benefit of the sector itself – the practitioners delivering services for children and families. This was a good example of the Ringelmann Effect (1913), the tendency for individual members of a group to become increasingly less productive as the size of their group increases. Ringelmann found as more people were added to a group, it often became increasingly inefficient. It is a useful counter-argument to those who believe big is better. To some extent, those one-and-a-half people back in 1995 arguably did more than the collective action of those 100 people ever could in 2005. The sweet spot was somewhere towards that journey when the team was of middle-size and functionality was much more effective. That may be an exaggeration, but not too far from the truth. Much cheaper as well, and made a better difference, with greater moral purpose. There surely ought to be an argument for some sort of solution in between these extremes of large and small, something in the middle of that.

Let's be realistic.

I love the phrase: turnover is vanity, profit is sanity, cash is reality. After over 25 years in business, I believe this is useful, with some justification. I have worked in the charity, voluntary and public sectors and I am well-used to the unfair accusation of being exclusively motivated by profit when working in the private sector. It's not their fault, all those business networking events and all the literature feeds that thinking. This of course is not only a simplistic view; it does not acknowledge we all have business missions and morals. The middle ground here is all that the different sectors in the business or charitable world have in common. All want sustainability, in charities we talk about reserves, in business the word is profit. The motives are the same, although the stakeholders are different. I say in early years and childcare (which is a highly diverse marketplace of international super-chains, chains of other sizes, individual nurseries or playgroups, home-based childminders and schools), it is not the name of the building, it is the quality of practice that matters. This means, we need to ensure the best possible quality services for children and not worry about who is delivering them.

Anyone in business appreciates the peace of mind and opportunities that money in the bank, generated by profit, offers. Let's face it, you could have an enormous turnover and be making a huge loss at the same time. And many businesses are in that exact position. Some of my most profitable years have been those when my business was smaller. I certainly know the huge difference that having financial resilience has on my own ability to be creative, confident and strategic. It releases all of those powers in abundance. The ability to build profits or reserves has been significantly under pressure for the past 10 years, after the financial crisis, and through a tough period of austerity funding, and rising delivery costs. It is time, again, to review, reconcile, and reason. US entrepreneur Mike Michalowicz explains these concepts well in his book Profit First (2017). And it reminds me of the story of the Brazilian village fisherman who was approached by a businessman who was sitting by the beach. He had watched the fisherman rowing his small boat towards the shore having caught a few large fish. The businessman asked *"How long does it take you to catch these fish?"*. *"Just a short while."* he replied. On the constant look out for growth and increased turnover, the businessman suggested the fisherman stay longer at sea and catch even more. The fisherman said he caught enough to feed his family, and it gives him time to go home and play with his children, have a nap in the afternoon with his wife, and then spend the evening with his friends playing guitar, singing and dancing. The businessman offered some ideas to be more successful. These were spending more time at sea, catching many more fish, building up some funds, and buying a bigger boat so even more fish could be caught. Then he could buy a whole fleet of boats, set up a fish processing plant and distribution network, move to the local city, set up a headquarters and manage several branches. *"And after that?"* asked the fisherman. *"After that, you can live like a king, then you can go public, float your shares, and become rich."* *"And after that?"* asked the fisherman. And here is the lesson. The businessman said, *"You can retire, move to the beach, catch a few fish, play with kids, have an afternoon nap with your wife, and in the evening join your mates for a drink and a party. The fisherman was baffled, "Isn't that what I am doing now?"* And there you have it, all that effort applied to achieve something already at reach. Not to mention the effects of the businessman's strategy on the sustainability of the local fish stocks and the depletion of a rural economy.

Let's let go.

Perhaps we could all embrace medium sized businesses and turnovers. Which means many will need to learn to let go, release the vanity and ego-boost attached to scale, and make some difficult and realistic decisions. Many businesses have not only survived, but they have also thrived, and look set to do very well indeed. Their growth is a real prospect. But some of those monumental structures in the financial districts of cities across the world are at risk of standing empty, or at least half full, as teams become smaller, tasks are automated, people continue to work differently, away from the office, and sometimes or always at home. Technology has accelerated the amount time we work remotely, virtually or on screen. The pressure now isn't about getting into work early and staying late, it is to be always on display. We are all living in our Truman Shows - at work, that is.

Try medium for size.

I think we could all be more interested in being more effective and positively impactful. And this is entirely possible in the middle, and in medium sized enterprises. We need to devote more time on meeting our stated aims and moral missions, to add value, and make the world a better place. And in the process, doing work effectively and meaningfully. We need to do this whilst sustaining ourselves, our teams and our workplaces at the same time. These are all the important things to do. Bigger isn't always better. Try the medium for size. Or even, dare I say it, be brave enough to be small. Now there's ego-free confidence. There's a good reason, there are plenty of big businesses who aren't there anymore, and plenty more clinging on. Their exponential growth fuelled by the financial mis-judgements accelerated by the Emperor's New Accountants. If they had been more modest, more middle, they might still be here, continuing to do good work, still employing people, supporting their supply-chains, and turning a decent profit to boot.

The high street needs middle-sized vision.

If middle sized businesses could be the answer, a good example of what I mean is found within the high street and retail industry. Another hat I wear is being co-owner of a retail shop selling homewares and furniture. This experience has shown me how the high street had become far too big. The past decades' financial greed and irresponsible investor led expansion has resulted in every high street looking and feeling the same. The same shop has been present in almost every high street, offering our towns and cities little or no point of difference. Instead, churning out a cynical, indistinguishable and predictable offer. All delivered with the chatter of scripted discourse prioritising mystery customer scores over and above the industry's proper objective of deriving real pleasure, real relationships, and real loyalty from actual customers enjoying authentic experiences. This does not connect with the shopper's demand and needs.

I have long thought this needed to stop. All of these recent experiences, can be used as the inspiration and stimulation for a new vision, direction, and plan.

Shame on those financiers, who had by all intents and purposes been hell-bent on foisting upon us this diluted high street offer - best described as 'retail average'. Their cynical experiment has failed or is failing. And shame on the landlords who have made things worse by levying extortionate rents, causing unsustainable 'here one day, gone the next' tenants.

The outcome is empty units, the same shops and brands all closed in great swathes. Ghosts of their former selves, the empty stores decaying where once trusted brands stood. Constant and concrete reminders of childhood Saturdays, memories of buying a first suit, and the excitement of furnishing a new home. Unsurprisingly, customers have roundly rejected much of it, or at best continued to down-grade their expectations and endure lack-lustre experiences. They feel uninspired, unsafe, and unvalued whilst the high street crumbles around them.

This sorry state of affairs must make way for a new offer, and big business still has a role to play in making that change happen. They should take the blame for what has happened and they must take the responsibility to create the necessary change. The doomsayers, who just don't understand the high street and what people want from it, need to alter their attitudes as well.

It's time for a new high street plan. It won't happen quickly, we will all have to be patient. The biggest opportunities for change are all about scale. There is big business on the high street, I have made that point, but most of it isn't. As a result, there is huge inequality and many of the sums just don't add up. First, we need to revise expectations around income, expenditure, rates and rent. They are so out of kilter. It is no wonder so many new start-ups struggle to make ends meet and are suspended in a hand-to-mouth state. It is also why the biggest retailers find themselves in huge financial holes, ones that their accountants think the way out of is to dig tunnels and not ladders to get out. Who is it in head office who thinks their bright ideas for huge flagship stores actually match the reality of customer demand? These are the very definition of vanity projects.

The supply chain is neglectful of small retailers. Wholesale suppliers need to be much more supportive of the smaller and middle sized independent traders, and not skewed to advantage the bigger players. They need to promote smaller orderings, affordable shipping costs, realistic credit control, and identify new ways of satisfying what customers want from their high street, online and order fulfilment services. Customers still want to see and experience products, to sit on them, try them on, smell them, and taste them. But they want to be able to take them home now or receive their no-hassle delivery efficiently and promptly. The sound business reason for this is that smaller retailers have the ability to grow into medium-sized ones. Trouble is once an independent becomes middle sized, some big players take them over with the aim of maxing them out.

The high street is not dead, nor is it dying, look carefully and can be reborn, if we think big and be brave enough to be middle sized about it. And like those local councils devoting their energies to restructuring their children's workforce all those years ago, too many are too slow to change.

Time to focus on managing in the middle.

Middle management occurs in a harsh environment. You've got to keep your eyes open. It is a corporate food chain, a pecking order, a desk filled chicken shed with a daily battle to see who is at the top of the roost. It's not just about chickens. Recently, whilst watching a nature programme on the television, the camera focused on the leader of a troop of baboons in the African bush. Snoozing on a branch of a tree in the heat of the midday sun, the baboon was unaware his likely successor was approaching. The narrator observed *"a leader should always sleep with one eye open."* He recognised baboons are not at the top of the food chain and they are not at the bottom. Risk and threat is everywhere, and can come from all angles. The narrator implied a leadership challenge was always a strong possibility when one is in such a position. That got me thinking about a whole bunch of things.

First, I started thinking about how middle managers can constantly feel being the target of challenge from those around them. And leaders may be fearful their successors are to be found in the middle, which may lead to feelings of distrust. That isn't a natural bedfellow of developmental leadership and management.

One of the terms and conditions of being any sort of leader or manager is you will be surrounded by any number of people with very firm and fixed views and opinions about how they could all do your job differently and/or better. Whilst this can feel draining and unwelcome, such challenges can be positive opportunities, they can hold us to account and keep us on our toes. It is a deep pool of ideas – one or two of them useful. These encounters and challenges can bring in new ideas and energy – we must be fully open to that. But they can also form a war of attrition on our motivation and position that makes it seem overwhelming. Making a difficult job, even harder.

I always say leaders and managers must be prepared and equipped to be under relentless scrutiny. You will be surrounded by colleagues who all think they could do a better job and then you will be bombarded with a whole raft of different ideas. If you were listening that is. This is a resource and motivating set of circumstances that need to be used for good.

But the reality can too often be unfair. The middle management role has significant restrictions and constraints. Middle managers rely on goodwill from those below them in the structure, and the reliable and full support of those above. Because it is those above that can often set up their middle management tier to fail. They don't intend to, but they do.

A great question to ask teams, is 'what would you do differently?' Teams are frequently overlooked resource and opportunity for innovation development. Be brave and ask. Sometimes it helps colleagues to learn decision-making and leadership is not as easy as they might think! Often, we can find an unwillingness of team members to get involved in these career building opportunities, and people recoil citing such activities are beyond their pay grade. Which is a lost learning opportunity for them and the middle manager. It also is one way of stagnating in a pay grade as the convincing evidence is not constructed for successful pay rise negotiations. All good advice for succession planning baboons out there.

People find succession planning difficult as it stirs up feelings of fear of loss of control, endings, and sometimes middle age anxiety in the workplace. Leaders must be prepared to leave or change or reinvent themselves when the time is right for them and the organisation. The trick is in knowing when that time is whenever it occurs. They should have one eye on who they are nurturing to replace them – that other baboon (and when and how), or how they attract or phase-in such a person into the organisation in readiness for when the time comes. They also need to prepare the team and organisation to willingly and warmly welcome such a person into the succession role. It can be a big wrench for team members loyal to the leader. If this promotes feelings of a lack of control for the leader, then there are likely problems ahead. Indeed, a good night's sleep will be far from possible.

This links to thoughts around the importance of personal wellbeing. Quality sleep is a serious matter and occupation for leaders, it impacts directly on mental and physical health in the short and longer terms. Revel in the thought your frontal cortex (responsible for executive functions such as planning for the future, judgement, decision-making skills, attention span, and inhibition) is having a break, and in the knowledge good sleep is believed to stave off a multitude of lifestyle diseases.

I used to call realistic professional perspectives 'work-life balance', but these days I am more focused on self-investment, and modelling such behaviours for those they lead. By that I mean anything from a long list of: self-development, lifelong learning, career evolution, personal physical health and emotional well-being, time to switch off and relax, and having a broad range of other non-work-related interests. The opposite of presenteeism; absenteeism. In the very best way. And just like in parenting, good pre-sleeping routines (not working, not looking at emails etc.) and a quality sleeping environment so that investment in sleep becomes an investment in self. Confident leaders should therefore sleep with both eyes firmly tight shut, and not have one eye on their inbox! They should also go on their holidays - and enjoy them. Allowing their colleagues to enjoy the break as well.

Middle is a fact of work.

Back to the workplace, and like a middle child, if you work in the middle or in middle management, you should think very carefully about how you fit into the order of things, and how you work with others from your middle position. You could ask yourself what it all means for you, including the position(s) you could adopt.

If you manage people in the middle (like a parent of a middle child), invest much more time and consideration and effort into thinking about their role and function and what you need to do to help.

If you are managed by a middle manager, then you ought to be equally concerned with the challenges middle management presents. As well as all this birth order stuff, you might also need to consider what structure is in your workplace. And how does age, in particular middle age, influence everyone's work behaviours. Middle is a fact of work. That's what this chapter is all about.

Managing middle management.

I have been the 'boss' for almost 30 years. That fortunate position means I have mostly avoided the particular challenge of being in middle management for a while. That said, I can often find myself occupying that horribly awkward position of balancing the needs of a client with those of a team member. Or caught in the middle between the tensions of colleagues, or on occasion two clients with opposing views and demands.

As my business grew larger in the mid-2000s, I have memories of having my own middle management tier underneath me. That didn't work so well at all. I really don't know why. I don't think we were immune to the Ringelmann effect ourselves. Remember that is when a team becomes too big and its efforts are disproportionately applied to managing itself. I did all I could to support, coach, promote autonomy, involve in and delegate decision-making, and set a framework for creative freedom. None of that worked. It seemed many in the middle didn't want to be there, and actually wanted something more directional in management and flatter in structure. By that I mean stronger, autocratic leadership with direct contact with all team members, rather than working through the line management structure. They may disagree. The most common fault I found at that time was the middle wasn't taking their own responsibility, and used me too frequently to defend their own actions or decision-making, or not. Phrases like *"James likes it done this way"*, or *"James expects or wants…"*. The reality was I hadn't expressed such preferences, instead I thought I was offering flexibility and autonomy, but somehow a mythical perception had grown and was being exploited. Truths were being created that simply weren't. That did not make me happy, or anyone else for that matter. It wasn't fair. When we became a smaller team from 2010, I took the opportunity to create a flatter structure that helped everyone hear what I was thinking and saying directly, without translation, interpretation, or manipulation. It worked, motivation increased, focus was sharpened, and openness and communication thrived.

In 2023, I sold the business to a group, and I have returned to the thrills of middle management, accountable to a board, a line manager, and finance and HR directors. Good job I was ready and prepared.

What do the managers of middle managers need to do?

The vast majority of people I have worked with when delivering leadership and management training courses are surprised to find themselves in their positions. Most have never undertaken any such training before. And they have learned their leadership skills through a painful process of trial and error. Like parenting a first child. That heady combination of instinct, a little reading, and masses of freely given, often unwelcome, and badly timed advice from everyone around you.

Perhaps there is more that leaders can do to change this culture by managing their middle management tier, better supporting them, and making their role more than bearable. If leaders aren't prepared to do that, they could get rid of the middle altogether and try doing the job themselves. Then they might realise what a challenging job it is.

What's needed here is plenty of coaching, so the middle managers are supported with what to say, and how to say it, and how they juggle all these competing demands and roles. Advice follows in this chapter.

Reinvent the middle.

Many of us are middle managers, and we all need to value, celebrate and embrace this important role. No one should view it as a steppingstone, or less important or valuable than the top jobs. The managers of middle managers need to invest more time and energy in them. Because middle management is extremely important to any organisation. If middle management fails, it is more likely the organisation will fail now or in the future.

We need those in the middle to feel great about it, and those above to understand it and stop making things worse through nervous or autocratic approaches. And those being managed by the middle need to play their part in making things better for everyone. It is thriving not surviving that should be the goal. But there is clearly an awkwardness about the whole issue. What could we do?

Middle managers are the secret to much success, and I think would benefit from some creative and exciting reinvention. If you're a middle manager, or you know one, or manage one, there are a few things I have learned along the way that I think are useful.

We could change our words.

If there is a problem with terminology and job titles, what could be a better alternative? My thinking is that job titles are fast becoming anachronisms. Relics of the workplace of the past, one of deep hierarchical and formal structures and inflexible often undemocratic functions. So, I'm quickly going off the idea of them altogether. I'm uncertain though as to what might replace them.

I remember earlier in my career I delighted in my first job titles. It made me feel all 'grown up' and they were obvious signs of my career progressing incrementally. I was so chuffed at the age of 27 years to bag the word 'senior' in my job title. How premature that seems now. Something I know I would recoil at these days, some decades later.

Call me senior today if you dare! That's the difference between young adulthood and middle age at work.

At work I've had the same job title for over 25 years, director that is. I have other project related titles, National this, Programme that, and I am a psychotherapist as well. In the latter role it is probably more justified to have such a title, like a doctor, for example. You wouldn't want to be operated upon by anyone without the words specialist or surgeon on their badge or CV would you? The same goes for a whole range of professions. But in general, modern work environments, we must ask if they necessary anymore. I'm not so sure.

Job titles do have a function. Like structures and hierarchies. They give the people you work with, internally and externally, including customers, the clues they need so they can work out what you do and tailor their interaction with you accordingly. It's the natural next step after they have consciously or subconsciously completed their initial assessment of you. You know, they've looked you up and down, checked out what you are wearing, and worked out how old or experienced or senior you are. They've analysed what you look like, sound like or instinctively feel like. They've assessed your age, class, ethnicity etc. Whether they realise it or not. And that is the problem, right there. That's exactly what people do. It is the work class test. The notion of class at work. Not working class, but class whilst working. And I'm fed up with it.

Remember Kierkegaard? He also said *"Once you label me, you negate me."* it is one of my favourite quotes, or at least the one I most easily use. The trouble with titles is they do squeeze people into small boxes. And in these egalitarian, flatter-structure, multi-tasking, nimble and fluid environments at work, who wants or needs to be so tightly defined? Not me. And I don't want the people I work with to be either. I want customers to be able to speak to any member of the team with confidence that their needs will be met. And for the customer to receive exactly the same service standard from anyone in the team. Top, middle, or bottom. That's why I think CEOs would benefit from sitting on reception, and not hiding away in their usual spot on the top floor, in the far corner, looking out of the window – usually the furthest place from the front door.

We can retune our thoughts and feelings.

Here are some helpful ways in which we can turn the common challenges of middle management into a killer job description:

What middle management usually experiences.

What middle management can do instead.

A feeling of having no place, and not fitting in.

Decide where you fit. Never miss an opportunity to tell people where that is, where you could be, and what difference you make. Become the Head of Joining Things Up.

Everyone wants you to do things.

Do be seen as the 'go to' person but be prepared to say no if it doesn't fit or someone else could be doing it. Don't fall into the trap of saying yes too often and doing everyone's dirty work. Become the Head of Getting Things Done.

You are overlooked in decision-making.	Do whatever you can to be involved in early pre-decision discussions, share ideas and proactively develop solutions to the problems you can see from your unique perspective. Become the Head of Constantly Making Useful Suggestions.
People question if you are needed.	Don't miss any opportunity to tell and show people what you are doing, and what effect and the impact you are having. Become the Head of Change Management and Communications.
You are trapped between the needs and demands of those at the top and those on the frontline.	Make and take time to listen, to acknowledge, to probe, to answer things you can, and to check-in that things are working. Become the Head of Happiness.
You are dumped with all the problems to solve, and the difficult conversations to have.	Swot up on conflict resolution theory and sales techniques. Become the Head of Problem Solving and Direct Communications.

We can change our behaviours and structures.

As we learned about the Ringelmann Effect, the big risk is that as organisations get bigger, roles become more separate, specialist and disconnected. If it isn't in your job description or title, then it simply isn't done. With larger teams, more specialist roles are often recruited for, with ever decreasing niched and nuanced person specifications. And if your role is also tightly defined, then the ability to work in a fluid and team-focused way can often, although not always, be stifled. It is the opposite of agile working. It is rigid instead. Specialisms and approaches start to create boundaries and blocks. Some aspects of job titles can be almost impossible to shake off. They limit change. And there is a huge risk of them reinforcing inequality and hierarchy and power. Which is the polar opposite of what we want to achieve in tackling privilege and opening up opportunity. I have seen colleagues painted into corners by virtue of holding administration roles and struggling to gain promotions because such a label is difficult to shake-off.

Middle managers can be expert listeners.

You, yes you, could be a great listener. You need to listen to those above and those below you - because everyone relies upon you to share and represent their thoughts, needs, and wants on their behalf. You need to accurately understand the leadership messages and expectations. You also need to represent the voice of the workforce correctly and fairly to the leadership team. And move all that data around afterwards.

We talk a lot about listening to children in early years and childcare. And I have always thought the best early years workers, social workers, and teachers are those that have excellent observation and listening skills. Whenever I am in a setting or school, I watch staff use visual and audible listening skills that can anticipate the individual needs of children and families. They are skills that can notice the unnoticed, the hidden, the unspoken, the subtext or bassline, and the things we are all trained to spot so we can safeguard children from harm. In psychotherapy, we listen to what is being said verbally, non-verbally, physically, and emotionally.

It is these skills that typify great leaders as well. If you notice what is being said and done, or what isn't being said or done, and consider how people are saying things and doing things, and how they are feeling, you have all the tools you need to connect with the people you lead, manage or serve.

For most leaders and managers, their route to the top is achieved by virtue of them being great talkers. But once there, the best advice is to *shut up!* If you are too busy talking at people, or seeking to demonstrate and constantly assert your position, you will not connect with them. You won't be able to listen either. Those you are working with will quickly learn not to talk themselves, which results in you becoming uninformed and out of touch with what is happening and how people feel. A recipe for disaster. Instead, learn to listen to understand, not just to craft your next smart or defensive reply.

In short, the worst leaders talk, the best leaders listen. If you want to find out more, there are lots of books and online resources that support good listening skills. Listening isn't as easy as it at first sounds, here are a few thoughts on how to listen well – containing my shortlist of personal tried and tested favourites.

-First of all, **listen to yourself.** What is your gut telling you? Review and reflect on the content of your journal, diary, or notebook.

-Don't start to listen when you've finished all your planning and are simply presenting your final ideas. **Start listening before you have begun.** Involve people early and listen at the early and middle stages of thinking or developing ideas.

-**Be open-minded** by not assuming what people are going to say before they say it. Otherwise, you will simply hear the things that reaffirm your expectations, the things that make you feel you were right. That is nice for you, but really isn't useful for everyone else.

-Listen to everyone, not just those that you know will agree, and be prepared for different views. Even if people say what you expect them to say. You might be surprised by the responses you get. And if you are avoiding asking some people, remember simply by asking their view and including it in your decision-making process, they may be much more supportive of it when implementation happens. That is called involvement, inclusion, and consultation.

-Be patient, give people time to think first and talk later, not everyone likes being the first to speak or thinks on their feet. Be prepared to hold a silence. Don't fill it yourself. You say enough already. Allow people the time to finish their talking – don't interrupt. Listen to those that talk last, they have had time to think and listen to everyone else.

-Repeat back what you think people have said so you get your listening right first time. **Accept that you don't always get it right the first time,** because when we are listening, we are also thinking at the same time – there's a lot going on. Ask probing and open questions.

-Listen without power. Support people to be honest and answer and not just in ways they think you want. If power is getting in the way, think about asking others to do the listening for you. I am thinking about other roles, or specialist researchers.

Middle managers can be expert acknowledgers.

You need to be an expert 'acknowledger'. Someone who can make everyone feel as if their needs, thoughts and feelings have been listened to, taken seriously, and will be used appropriately - as and when the right moment arises. This is the difference between being listened to and feeling listened to. There is a huge difference.

Maya Angelou, US poet and civil rights activist, is often quoted. Rightly so. She said *"I've learned that people will forget what you said, people will forget what you did, but people will never forget how you made them feel"*. This is good advice for any manager or leader. It reminds me of the big difference between leadership and management. Leaders inspire people to have confidence and take action themselves. Managers too often tell people what to do, how and when. And this can damage confidence, motivation, and individual responsibility. Don't get me wrong, we need both in every organisation. Often it is the same person. Sometimes it has to be that way. It could be you, and if it is, this is your juggling challenge that makes every workday different. You can lead and manage in the middle very successfully. Good advice is to consider if you are a leader or a manager, or both, and to carefully and considerately develop your plan of action.

Middle managers can be expert talkers.

You also need to be a great communicator. This is because you are the conduit or channel of messaging up and messaging down. You need to share information in ways adapted to different audiences and be able to motivate action in the process. These are the skills of the diplomat and the marketeer – skills of the middle child in actual fact. This is all about style, nuancing the message, timing, and finessing communication in ways that are attractive and acceptable to the receiver. This is because middle managers are agents of change and negotiation – so everyone is happy.

Middle managers can be change experts.

By having such a role, a middle manager needs to know the processes for making change happen, and the emotional responses people have to it. As you know, I like the Kubler Ross theories and charts around grief and change. Because grief is not always about death, but it is always about endings. And there are plenty of new beginnings and endings in business. The charts are a useful addition to any middle manager's toolbox or back pocket. You can plot where people are in the process, and look at the next up and comings stages – then your strategies can be developed

"I've learned that people will forget what you said, people will forget what you did, but people will never forget how you made them feel."

———○———

Maya
Angelou

and applied using this awareness and information more effectively. They help pinpoint the feelings of shock, denial, frustration, anger, bargaining, depression and acceptance in processing endings. Sounds sensible and simple enough, but it isn't.

If one thing is for certain in any business environment, it is change. The workplace has transformed almost from all recognition. The effects of technology, have all driven change in predicted and unforeseen ways. Take a breath and celebrate this change, and your success in making it work, before you read on. And take from that, whatever change happens in the future, you have the skills to lead and survive it!

Middle managers and those around them need to reach a position where change is embraced, and adopt a 'can do' approach to making it work. Sometimes we can see change coming, or it can take us by surprise. The middle role must support all of those around, up and down, to travel positively and safely through change before, during and after it happens. Without effective management, change can be stalled, damaging, unsettling and stressful. It needs a considered and inter-personal approach that is built upon some tried and tested structures and models. This is because we all have emotional and organic responses to changes, and this varies according to a whole raft of individual reasons that are affected by our role, experience, qualifications, health, personal life, and personal goals and ambitions. Natural responses to change include feelings of: anger, depression, fear and pessimism; as well as excitement, happiness and optimism. The potential for work-related stress is real and therefore ups the importance of sound management.

Middle managers can know timing is everything.

A key message is that we all operate on different timescales. Some of us will adopt change more quickly. Rogers Adoption Bell Curve in the 1950s showed us how different people respond to innovation. The first to get on board are the natural innovators. The ones that relish the risk and newness of change. They like to engage in trial and error. After them come the early adopters. They have looked with interest at the successes and mistakes of the innovators, and take the best of what they have learned. In their wake come the early majority. Now we have a real sense of a movement of change as more people come on board. We have reached the tipping point, and the late majority now join the party. Last but not least come the 'laggards' as Rogers describes them. That's not a great word that, I prefer something more positive. I suggest 'deep-thinkers', or 'the rest', not that the others don't think, but the ones to join last are likely the ones that really wanted and needed to think things through, observe and evaluate, and take time to make considered plans and actions. Some people do need time to think things through before they accept it. Much to the frustration of the impatient fast decision-makers around them, otherwise known as the 'doers'. And there is nothing more annoying to them than being with someone who is really super-keen about risky change very early if you are still on the journey! Whichever way try to avoid wasting time fighting things that will not change and you have no control over. You won't enjoy it, you will drain your energy and it will be very frustrating. Every team needs someone from each category. That creates balance.

The response will depend on several factors which include: is the change fairly minor and being suggested by staff or leadership? Is it a major strategic change which is being externally imposed, for example the introduction of new legislation? At what speed is the change being introduced? Is there a common enemy that might garner some sort of coalition? Timing is key. Informed by the best listening skills, acknowledging techniques, communication, diplomacy and tact, and a good grounding in change management theory. There you go – that is the essential survival guide if you are in middle management.

Middle managers need to 'own it'.

Key to success in the middle is the ability to be confident enough to 'own' the message and to not blame colleagues or leadership when things get tricky. I have set out my personal experience of clearly setting out goals and actions (A), and working these through with a middle management tier (B), only for these to be reinterpreted and reinvented by the time they reach the rest of the team (C). There's nothing simple in that ABC and little else that is so infuriating or frustrating. The result in this disconnect is contradictory messaging, a breakdown in trust, confusion and demotivation caused by uncoordinated messages. Middle managers need delegated responsibility and the freedom and permission to develop decisions with the team. That has the potential for better ownership and incentive.

Middle managers can understand and use boundaries.

Now there have been times in my life when work has got in the way of life, I have had work-life imbalance and I have suffered. Remember, those times when I said yes too often. I didn't have time to pursue all other interests. But those days are long gone – thankfully.

If people are thinking retirement isn't for them, I think it's most probable there is an imbalance in their work and life now. Work is a little too important. Are they fearful there will be a similar imbalance in their retirement? Either way there are boundary issues for me. I think it is vital we have boundaried work and life identities. I have not met anyone in their later years who told me they wished they had worked more. Indeed, the opposite is the case. There are exceptions to this rule, and this is where the idea of vocations come in. A vocation being that strong feeling of suitability or commitment to a particular career or occupation. It depends upon the work someone does and their moral conviction, these can drive long and extended periods of work. Sometimes the boundaries can be blurred between the work self and the home self. Especially if you live where you work, think a vicar living in the vicarage, or a shopkeeper living upstairs, for example. What is important is rest and healthy working, so the work is done, but the self is also supported and nourished.

It is essential to hold your boundaries at work, at the top, middle and the bottom. In the middle you are landlocked and have more boundaries to defend than the others. In the middle, one must be confident, or at least effectively project your confidence. No one knows how you are feeling unless you tell them, or when you leak your feelings intentionally or accidentally. If you're getting these things right and you are showing confidence it helps make sure everyone appreciates that is where you are – in the middle. For better or for worse. You must hold the middle boundary. If leadership starts to feel your allegiances are downward focused, or colleagues think the opposite it could be the recipe for many problems. Stick your flag in the middle ground, be consistent, clear, principled, and loyal to all. Tell people what it is like in the middle, explain the dilemmas and thought processes openly and clearly. That way I think you stand the chance of getting more support and understanding. When you start to not like it, the middle that is, move. Go up or down, sideways or somewhere else. A reluctant middle manager without a confident position and situation is not a happy middle manager. And that will only result in disappointed top management and unhappy workers.

Middle managers can iron out creases.

Finally, be able to mediate. To resolve conflicts. Like middle children, they are the in-house diplomats and negotiators. Once you have supported everyone to consider different viewpoints and navigate change, use mediation and problem-solving techniques to ensure everyone feels acknowledged, listened to, understood, and part of the solution.

A huge part of being a middle manager is managing complaints and disagreements. It may be one of the aspects of your role that you dread. Some thrive on it; loving the opportunities to listen, and support others to reach resolutions. In some organisations, they devote whole teams to managing complaints. In most small and medium sized businesses there isn't that luxury. Someone to take over these difficult scenarios. Actually, they rarely do a good job. It's so impersonal. So, it's yet another one of those things we must all do in the middle. We must be multi-skilled.

What is absolutely clear, is each and every middle manager can have strategies up their sleeves to deal with them. Complaints often come without warning. Sometimes you can see them brewing. More often than not, they present themselves when you are busy doing something else. And they come from all directions, they can come from the top leadership and the workforce below. One thing is for sure, the middle manager always seems to be in the firing line. So, knowing how to structure a response to a complaint, without making it worse in the short-term, is an essential part of the middle manager's toolbox. It is part of team leadership, customer care, and time management as well.

What's worked for me is something I picked up when training customer care staff in the tour operator world. And a useful way to remember it is APAC, which stands for acknowledge, probe, answer, and close/confirm.

I think that acknowledging a person's complaint, anger or upset is the single most effective strategy of all. We've already identified the need for super-strength acknowledging skills in the middle. Demonstrating you have heard the complainer, and you believe they have a point will show you are not going to argue. This will support them to move their energies away from trying to convince you, and instead move to working with you to tell you more. Fail to acknowledge and they may get angrier, louder, more aggressive, or frustrated. And both of you will be going nowhere fast. You will start to resent the time this is taking, and which other important things it is preventing you from getting on with.

And it is the second stage, probe, where both sides, but especially you, can ask for some of the facts that will support you to understand in detail about the problem or the events leading to it. Through this stage your well-practised listening, body language and empathy can show how you are likely to respond with something serious and considered thoughts. Including the word 'yes' frequently during the acknowledgement and probing will also help.

Then give your response. But make sure you give yourself sufficient time to think, so you don't rush into saying things you don't mean or will regret. This may be a few moments, a few minutes or even hours or days if this is appropriate. But in the heat of the moment, phrases like 'let me think about that for a second' explains to the complainant that your silence isn't empty or unhelpful, but about you carefully considering what they have said, and what you are going to do. That this is different and deserves a bespoke, not off the shelf reply. There is an opportunity for them to think about what they could do. To take ownership of their own resolution.

Close is all about gaining agreement your answer is okay or acceptable. If not, start with APAC again, acknowledge you haven't got things right, and probe some more, then return to reiterate or replace the answer, before reaching the close again. Hopefully with better results.

It sounds like a lot of hard work, but it is an exciting and essential role thinking about it.

The new middle at work.

The middle space and middle workforce in any organisation is hugely important aspects in the work environment. Its role is influenced and affected by all the common features of the middle. It is all about order and fitting it, and how we are expected tacking and allowed to perform in that space. Sound familiar to you middle-children out there? There are particular skills and qualities needed to survive in the middle. And as a society and a business world we must rethink, repurpose and revalue the middle. Business needs to reconsider its relationship with scale. To let go of ego inflating bigness and be brave enough to enjoy and aim for success in the middle. To do that we could value, invest in and nurture our middle managers and help them to thrive not merely survive.

—o—

The middle ground

> **"There is a fifth dimension beyond that which is known to man... It is the middle ground between light and shadow, between science and superstition, and it lies between the pit of man's fears and the summit of knowledge."**

———o———

**The Twilight Zone,
TV series.**

Taking your position.

Hopefully, by now we are all on board with middle ideas and their qualities, characteristics, and quirks. The middle ground is no exception and can be found in all aspects of our lives. It is the place between all things, and this chapter focuses on politics, our views, and opinions – and risks and opportunities. Of course, all of that is influenced and informed by our various middles.

Despite our best intentions, sometimes we find ourselves in positions and situations we weren't expecting to be in, or we didn't really want. Being in the middle can take you by surprise, you might not have seen it coming, but in an instant there you are, stuck, caught, and in the middle of a hot mess.

We may find ourselves awkwardly sandwiched or between two or more sides, older or younger siblings, superiors or juniors, competing agendas, conflicting arguments, and various opinions or beliefs. Whether that be in our early, middle, or later lives, at home or work, or when out and about in wider society with friends and others. Those moments when we find ourselves in the middle at work, can be career-defining, career-ruining, or career-cul-de-sac moments. Before you know it, you are having to apply all those things you have learned in the middle. It is a real test. All of our varied middle experiences have shown it's not easy trying to please everyone all of the time. You've been asked to officiate or mediate, or you're getting involved between two diametrically opposed positions, or even worse asked to share your own view – one that runs the risk of upsetting some and pleasing the others. Indeed, having an opinion at work these days can be troublesome. For some people it has gotten them irretrievably labelled, damaged, or cancelled. Middle children may be skilled at seeing such predicaments coming, as they are more likely to have honed their ability to notice the pre-signs, in readiness of the need to facilitate conflict resolution, or to conveniently keep their head down, and they may build better relationships and careers as a result.

Adopting the middle position may be a deliberate choice, and some (like Robin The Frog) have found being in the middle to be a place of sanctuary and peace. All of these situations open up the choice to adeptly adopt the middle position.

So then, we have the middle ground, and that is the focus of this fifth and final main chapter. The fifth dimension.

Politics and the middle.

When it comes to politics, I don't think there is enough middle. It's all too split. Another false choice between one or the other, red and blue, or blue and red – leaving a massive gap in between. As Janet Street Porter, one of my favourite English broadcasters and journalists, said: *"...the big hole in British politics remains in the centre"*. So much so that our middling liberal political leader, Ed Davey resorted to dare-devil stunts to gain any sort of attention in the 2024 general election, including paddleboarding, arriving at the party conference on a jet-ski, and releasing a Christmas single amongst very many others.

Two party politics does little to promote harmony and reasonable behaviours across all of our society, and in legislature. In the US, the east and west coasts are Democratic party leaning or dominated - they are blue. In the middle, there is a much stronger leaning to red, for the Republicans. In the UK, we have the red (Labour) with a dominance in the north and urban areas, and the south and rural leaning blue (Conservatives), with a smattering of smaller parties. Apologies to those, but we must admit this is currently a two-party battle. The two main parties sit facing and staring and shouting at each other in the Houses of Parliament. They try to convince themselves, and us, of their inherent differences, when sometimes there isn't much difference to be had at all. It is a tribal battleground of political urbanity that only seems to serve those who are entangled in it. It does little to connect and engage with the unrepresented middle which is where the numbers every politician needs. Indeed, it is the cleverest of politicians who know the how to woo the middle - and to listen to them, and realise the elite class, are a minority in voting terms. And all that causes the political map to swing like a pendulum from one to the other every few years or so. A change mostly as a result of the electorate's growing disdain for the ruling party, long-term memory loss, and believing the opposition may be given a chance, all in the vain hope they will be better or different.

The right to vote?

Some people ask whether everyone be given the vote at all. They think the electorate cannot be trusted to vote how they would want them to. It is this sort of mentality and vice like grip on power that stopped women and the working class having the vote in the first place. The elite don't like it when the majority votes go the other way.

Only 58% of adult men were eligible to vote in England before 1918. That year, women over the age of 30 who met a property qualification (middle and upper classes in the main) were entitled to vote for the first time, that was about two-thirds of the adult female population. I am sure it was customary in those days for their husbands (or fathers) to instruct them who to vote for. The same act (Representation of the People Act 1918) extended the vote to effectively all men over the age of 21 years (19 for men in the armed forces). These reforms saw the electorate surge from eight to 21 million. A huge letting go of historical, institutional, and class privilege. Yet inequality between women and men remained enormous. It was not until 10 years later and the Equal Franchise Act (1928) that women aged over 21 could vote with the same legal rights as men.

Much hasn't changed. There is still tension. The ruling classes, the elite, are a minority, and it is the middle and working classes that are the majority. Today in democratic countries, the losers of elections still retain the instinct to mistrust the electorate. Losers have started to claim either popular or moral victory - or both. Look at US President Trump, he claimed victory in 2017, Hilary Clinton claimed victory in the same election. She got the most votes, but the electoral college system generated the Trump victory. Four years later and Trump's position was in reverse. Four years after that and he became only the second president, after Grover Cleveland, to return to office after a one-term break.

UK Labour leader Jeremy Corbyn lost a general election in December 2019 (said to be the worst result for Labour in decades), yet it was reported he claimed victory in principle as his policies were highly popular.

We have witnessed the overt and unspoken debates on the value of some people's votes being worth more than those of others. For me it only serves to highlight the distance between the political policy makers, the voters they are seeking to tempt, and the population they are tasked with serving. It exposes their lack of understanding, their delusion, and their distrust or oversight of the middle and working classes. Who, in turn, return the compliment in spades - they don't like politicians back.

It seems the right to vote is only okay when the vote is right.

Politics and the working class.

My attention was grabbed by a poll that highlighted this tension between political messaging and the priorities of the working class voter. Until then I hadn't been aware of the special interest group that commissioned it, the Campaign for Common Sense. The message focused upon how local priorities are founded on directly material issues like street crime or employment, rather than more abstract (yet important) policy and moral debates about identity, politically correct language, or cancel culture. All of which seem to become important only when someone had a direct link to it or felt the impact of it. Although, there are signs the general public is tolerant, fair, and moderate. In contrast, the political or social narrative often paints a different picture. It made me link the idea of 'common sense' to the 'common man/person', more politely known as the working-class electorate. I've heard people say they have common sense and don't need to study, or that educated people don't have common sense even though they are qualified.

Politicians have a tendency to sneer at simple and straightforward thinking, preferring instead to wrap it up with complicated detail - which is a class issue. They say, 'let me be clear' and then tie their rhetoric up in knots, not being clear at all. Where does this feature in the middle I wonder? Politicians (in the minority) do have a basic obligation to represent the views of their constituencies (the majority). This isn't always applied. Our politicians are perceived as being the elites, not listening, and not experiencing real life in the same way as their constituents. There are moral dilemmas when the majority view isn't right morally, ethically, or even legally. And many MPs have been caught in the crossfire and confusion of both representing diametrically opposed views of their constituency, and their own opinions, whilst frequently not representing any of them at all.

The B Word.

Now let's contemplate Brexit and its relationship with the middle. Well, it doesn't have one – take it from me. The UK's European Union (EU) referendum held in 2016, artificially required the British public to choose yes or no, to choose in or out. We were asked whether we wanted to stay in the EU or leave it. The architects of the referendum built their scheme upon what turned out to be a very wobbly foundation indeed. Their motivation was to placate the far right and grumpy backbench MPs once and for all. They hoped they would put the issue to bed. The government believed the vote to remain would win outright. It didn't. What at first seemed like a political folly, an excuse to travel the nation in a campaign bus and engage in school-debating-society standard discourse, whilst indiscriminately scattering unfounded promises, actually ended up having far from silly consequences. Vote remain received 48.1% and vote leave won with 51.9%.

Not exactly a convincing result. A truly split decision. That was a shock to the top of government, and to many of us – it still is. For me, the chatter on the streets was much more in favour of leaving than the ruling classes were prepared to acknowledge, let alone to contemplate or imagine. It resulted in the immediate resignation of the Prime Minister, David Cameron. And it was a result that reverberated throughout society and created a multitude of ongoing political quandaries and casualties ever since. It split families, saw the breakup of relationships and marriages, ended long-held friendships, and closed or compromised businesses. On balance it probably created some new ones. The irony was the same prime minister had commissioned a £2m happiness survey to measure and monitor the well-being of society. I guess the results of that weren't easy reading.

I think if a middle choice had been available in the referendum, that would or could have been a much better prospect for all of us, perhaps even something that was a comfortable, sensible and a unifying option.

English author Nick Hornby's State of the Union was published in 2019, three years after the EU referendum. I didn't read the book,

I watched it on the television instead. Hornby expertly and adeptly conflated the notion of Brexit with the trials of a marital relationship. His premise was a married couple (Louise and Tom) meet in a pub each week, immediately before their marriage counselling session. In the pub, over a pint and a glass of wine, they reviewed the week and prepared for the therapeutic session ahead. We never joined them in the counselling room, instead each episode ended with them going inside. The result of the 2016 EU referendum became a live issue during episode two. Brexit was about divorce, rather than a relationship, the metaphor was reconciliation. A brutal and uncompromising split between two long term partners (Britain and the rest of Europe). Louise accidentally discovered Tom voted out. She voted in. He admits to being motivated to wind-up her friends with his vote. She shares her concerns that we would lose all our East European (public and hospitality) servants – care workers and health workers, as a result. Very much an unashamedly middle class perspective. She didn't seem to appreciate the irony.

Overall, Brexit was a disastrous process, regardless of your own view or choices. The result could have been much better constitutionally prepared for. Its implementation continues to drag on, and its impact has cast a long-shadow after that. But the root of that lack of forward planning was that dyed-in-the-wool tendency to overlook the middle. The Government's blinkered view was that the result would be one and not the other, not something opposite to that or a sentiment in between. The majority was far too small for such a massive and disruptive undertaking. A greater majority should have been required, and perhaps other democratic tests to be passed afterwards as part of the process.

On that sunny spring morning, as I walked along the main street of my village, in the middle of England, I thought anything could happen. I voted remain. I could've easily voted to leave. I was caught in the middle and nearly didn't vote at all. I never thought I would abstain a vote – but recently this has been quite a regular feature of my democratic self. It has started to become a greater consideration and habit for me and I can see a long-term pattern emerging. I agree with Street Porter again: "...*like a lot of decent people in the middle I now have nobody to vote for.*"

I didn't stay up to watch the result, thinking 'what will be, will be'. It was too close to call. But when I saw the result on my 'phone through bleary eyes, squinting without my glasses the next morning, I gasped with shock. A rude awakening indeed. I respected the result. Something that has been very hard for a lot of people to do. That is democracy, it isn't perfect, but I cannot think of a reasonable alternative. The majority view is not always right though, but it is democratic. Early on I was left with no firm and fixed view whether the EU referendum result was the right or wrong one. There's already a slew of research and reports that assert slower economic growth, fewer jobs, raised costs of living, and shortages of medical supplies for example. As a business owner, I know we have really suffered with the consequences.

Intolerant liberalism.

All the ensuing post Brexit debate focused upon the small differences of the voting patterns. Young people blamed older people for voting out, older voters criticised the young for voting remain. The liberal elite, you guessed it, blamed the 'ignorant', uninformed working classes. It became a race issue as well, as people conflated the idea that leaving the enormous governing and bureaucratic structure of the EU was racially motivated. It was in part, but not in totality.

Curiously, the idea of liberalism is at risk of being associated with privilege and control. Quite the irony. This philosophy, often criticised for its impractical position, could instead be a key to open a new door. John Stuart Mill said *"to be liberal is to be imperfect"*. He defended in On Liberty (1859) all our rights to speak, and do things as we wish, as long as we are aware of our imperfections – still good advice. Tolerance, liberalism, and cancel culture are not natural bedfellows. *"Sometimes in being blindingly liberal you end up as a contradiction of yourself by creating another rigid narrative"* said Boy George. Middle has the capacity to become the modern liberalism, the new liberalism, given half a chance.

"Sometimes in being blindingly liberal you end up as a contradiction of yourself by creating another rigid narrative."

———o———

Boy George

Genocide.

Ignorance, fear, and power are the essential ingredients for extreme actions on national and international scales. A recent and tragic example is Rwanda, which featured direct, indirect, and institutional racism. Almost one million people were murdered during a 100-day period in 1994. The conflict was between two 'groups': the Hutus and the Tutsis. The ethnic tensions that underpinned the conflict, originated from the time when Rwanda was a Belgian colony. The Belgians created not just ethnic but also class divides by favouring the Tutsis, who were given privileges and roles to support the administration of the country. Tutsis were taller, had lighter skin and were believed by the Belgians to be 'more elegant' than Hutus. For many citizens, including the colonists, it was difficult to always recognise the distinctions between two socially and artificially defined class based or aesthetically informed ethnicities. The Belgians unbelievably measured the width of people's noses, to determine ethnicity; Tutsis were those with narrower ones. Characteristics were listed on people's ID cards. This preferential treatment, unjust categorisation, and the subsequent benefits that Tutsis enjoyed (such as employment, money, class and social advantage) understandably built-up resentment in the excluded Hutu communities. When the Belgians departed in 1962, they left the Hutu majority in power. Once the power imbalance had been reversed, extremists in the Hutu community plotted and sought revenge on their decades of oppression. And when the president was assassinated during the civil war, there was a power vacuum, and the opportunity was taken. Hutus murdered hundreds of thousands of Tutsis, people they thought were Tutsis, and some of the Hutus that stood in their way. People were murdering their next-door neighbours. We all have next door neighbours – can you imagine any conditions that would drive you to such actions? Controversially, the developed world did nothing to stop the bloodbath. A common feature of genocides I have found. History tells us that despite a level of awareness, electronic news media, and

United Nations resources, the rest of the world stood by, and dismissed the genocide as yet another 'third world incident'.

Less than 20 years after the genocide and I was in Kigali, the capital of Rwanda. I was on the way to spend time in the forests with mountain gorillas. I visited the genocide museum. It was difficult to reconcile the events of 1994 with what I was seeing around me. A bustling city getting on with its business. But I know the effects of trauma when I see them. This was clearly evidenced in the museum, but there was an unspoken sense of quiet in that community. Probably still contemplating and internalising the horrors that had fallen upon them and their friends and families. It will take generations for the population to recover economically, socially, and emotionally. On that day, I wrote in my travel journal: *"Man's intolerance and ability to create conflict, death and hate out of nothing, just astounds me"*.

I am not sure it is out of nothing. What happened in Rwanda was the product of centuries of class division, social conditions, colonialism, privilege, and inequality. This all built up, like little jigsaw pieces to complete the picture and create the tragedy that occurred.

In 2020, I travelled to Cambodia. And there I found another example of how social class (not ethnicity alone) had been used to promote murderous effects. The communist Khmer Rouge movement, led by Pol Pot, was motivated, in part, by perceptions of economic injustice, and exploitation of the poor, uneducated, and rural farmers. The violence and political dogma sought to redress balance. The enemy was to be exterminated and that enemy was the ruling middle classes.

The three million that died between 1975 and 1979 were categorised by the Khmer Rouge as the middle classes – the liberal elite, and intellectuals. The wearing of glasses, implying intellectualism and relative wealth, were enough to send people to death. I visited security prison 21 (S-21) in Phnom Penh, the capital of Cambodia, now another museum. A former secondary school where classrooms had been converted into interrogation and torture centres. The school was a holding area for people before they were sent, stripped naked, to the killing fields to die. A very moving place, that did nothing to reduce my thoughts and feelings about the brutality of secondary schools. There I met someone who as a child who had been photographed on liberation day. He was called Norng Chan Phal, and about my age. He was found, aged nine-years-old hiding underneath in a pile of the clothes left behind by naked prisoners being bussed to the killing fields. He lost both of his parents in the genocide. Norng was now a Khmer Rouge historian and political analyst. I bought his book and shook his hand. Tears welled in my eyes. I was literally touched by the experience of genocide. It felt completely current, real, and utterly possible again.

The standout thoughts for me about my experiences in Rwanda and Cambodia are that such extraordinary and hugely damaging events seem so achievable and possible within what we might describe as 'normal' society. They are driven by the class system, and other social factors and forces. And how small perceptible and imperceptible differences were used. Ones familiar to us all in day-to-day life. And then as fast as these horrific events occur, they stop, and life carries on in some way afterwards. The roots, I think, of these atrocities are familiar to us all in terms of attitudes towards difference, intolerance of others, inequality, and organised actions. It reminds me of when I was in Hiroshima in 2000, 55 years after the US dropped a nuclear bomb on the city, and on Nagasaki three days later (an incident often overlooked). One 1998 study found over 200,000 people died, half of them on the day. When I was there, like when I was in Kigali, everyone was getting on with their lives. I visited the peace park and looked at the horror depicted in the photographs. When I arrived, I had imagined and hoped such a horror would never be repeated. I left with one thought. That this unthinkable devastation could easily happen again.

After my Rwandan visit, I was motivated to look at the stages that took communities towards genocide. Now you may not at first easily link issues of class to genocide. But it is about how we classify people. According to the Holocaust Memorial Day Trust, the 10 steps to genocide are:

1. Classification - The differences between people are not respected. There's a division of 'us' and 'them' which can be carried out using stereotypes or excluding people who are perceived to be different. This is familiar territory in most societies.

2. Symbolisation - This is a visual manifestation. In different cultures we all have our own symbols. The way we dress, our jewellery, our hair styles. They all indicate our differences and can become the focus hatred.

3. Discrimination - The dominant group denies civil rights or even citizenship to identified groups. This is common if there are high levels of refugees, asylum seekers, and population migration.

4. Dehumanisation - Those perceived as 'different' are treated with no form of human rights or personal dignity. Denigratory language is used to describe different people and it drives the behaviours of oppressors.

5. Organisation - Demonstrations and riots aren't always planned, but they often are. Regimes of hatred often train those who go on to carry out the destruction of a people. There's talk that the Rwandan events were planned for over a year before they happened.

6. Polarisation - Propaganda begins to be spread by hate groups. We all know the news media is controlled by a small group of individuals, all with their own and deliberate agendas, we have seen this balloon as social media facilitates all sorts of unmoderated and polarised viewpoints.

7. Preparation - Perpetrators plan. They often use euphemisms such as the Nazis' phrase 'The Final Solution' to cloak their intentions. They create fear of the victim group, building up and motivating 'armies' and weapons.

8. Persecution - Victims are identified because of their ethnicity, class, or religion and death lists are drawn up. People are sometimes segregated into ghettos, deported, or starved, and property is often expropriated. Genocidal massacres begin.

9. Extermination - The hate group murders their identified victims in a deliberate and systematic campaign of fear and violence.

10. Denial - The perpetrators or later generations deny the existence of any crime.

I read these stages and realised that they happen, again and again and again. They are happening now, using this framework you will notice it frequently. The Holocaust Memorial Day Trust asserts identity-based persecution takes place daily across the world. I came to realise how often I was confronted with its reality when travelling on holiday, I wasn't deliberately seeking these examples out but they are easily there to find.

The steps to genocide 1-3 are relevant on a day-to-day basis, those being class, symbolisation, and discrimination. I revisited them when we were at the height of Brexit in the UK, and time and again when there has been social unrest or cultural schisms. In the summer 2024 UK riots, the newspapers reported that people were being stopped in their cars to be asked if they were White British so to allow them safe passage.

Dithering decision making.

Personally, when considering my voting intentions, I would describe me as 'dithering' over Brexit. I had done my utmost to filter out and cast aside the racist nature of some of the clumsy and toxic anti-immigration campaigning narrative. Because I am convinced, and I am strongly of the opinion, that it is entirely possible to be a Brexiteer and not be anti-Europe or indeed nationalistic or racist. I know others will disagree. Even though immigration was a top issue for leave voters (Ipsos Mori June 2016), one can have concerns over the detail of immigration policy and not be racist as well. But it is a complex matter. The electorate can reject an overburdensome, authoritarian, bureaucratic super-government, and not be racist or anti-European. There is a lovely big world out there to connect with too. Europe very much included.

If there had been middle ground here, it would have sated the thirst of people who wanted to stay, on the condition of reform, or a (re)negotiated relationship with the EU. That option simply wasn't on the ballot paper. That was a REAL shame.

In very many ways, democracy causes us to all attach to and adopt binary and divided positions. It asks us to vote one of two ways, additional and niche or alternative candidates aside. There isn't enough middle ground, no finely finessed terms. Some might think this an impossibility – an unrealistic goal, but the ballot box is far too rigid for my liking. This is contributing to voter apathy, including mine. Just look at turnout rates (for the EU referendum it was 72.2%). Which means that a mere 37.5% of the eligible voting population voted to leave – yet 100% of us had to. We are being coerced into being red or blue, in or out. The battleground of the surrounding campaigns, including stage-managed TV debates, are just farcical. In the run up to the EU referendum, there was a plethora of fake manifesto commitments from people of all parties who had no authority to give or deliver such promises●

Traditionally, the working class is Labour, the aspirational working and the middle classes and elites are Conservative. But boundaries are blurred. Politicians attach themselves to class identity to suit their message(s). Some say they were working class, and now they are middle. Some say they are middle for the middle. One even claimed they became working class when they took a summer job in a famous fast-food restaurant. A former PM once contradicted himself as he boasted he had *"friends who were working class, well not working class"*.

Things have changed. Voting intentions and poll results flip and flop. The long-held multi-generational voting traditions are broken, in parallel to the shifting sands of class. Whole constituencies have shed their allegiances and loyalties in favour of the 'other side'. Red can become blue on the political map, blue can become red. Basic colour theory would suggest we all consider becoming a little more purple. I learned that at art school you know.

What is happening, it seems to me, is that the opposites are becoming more extreme and further and further apart. That will do two things. It will make them smaller (on both sides) and it will make the middle bigger. That then, becomes the power base of the future. Politicians and the community could understand that and use it as a force for good. For now, it all seems to be an unsettling 50:50 split.

The Brexit vote generated such division and hatred during and after the campaign, and we know how dangerous that can be. I frequently Googled steps to genocide at the height of the pre-Brexit debate and during its fall out. I felt things could get nastier than they actually were already. They did. It led to the murder of Jo Cox MP, when she was arriving at her constituency office. Her murderer was a right-wing extremist. This heinous act was a stage four event, the fatal consequence of the dehumanisation of a politician. She wasn't the last serving MP to be killed at work, and I fear she will not be the last. In the 2024 US presidential election I started to lose count of the apparent assassination attempts on Trump. That was an election campaign we were told was too close to call. Given the convincing result in favour of Trump, I wonder if people were telling the pollsters the truth, and I read that many voters weren't even telling their friends and family of their voting intentions. I guess that's another sign of the division I have written about, in the form of relational breakdown, separation and divorce, and neighbourhood disputes.

We need much more compromise, compassion, and concord to counter such toxic polarised views and opinions. This isn't about being opinion-less. It needn't feel dispassionate or uncommitted. We all need to be able to appreciate all views and delight in occupying the middle space. We don't have to be angry or outraged or insulted. We can be happy, tolerant, and confident in the middle.

Social media isn't helping.

Social media is something increasingly integrated into personal and professional lives. I use it in a professional capacity to highlight best practice, share news and information, and to highlight information about what is happening in my field. The need for best behaviour and boundaries has never been bigger.

Social media is a hugely seductive space, it is irresistible to most, and easily facilitated by emerging and ever-evolving devices and algorithms. As a result, our inner self-promotion and editorial urges are becoming out of control. We are social animals, and we are being tooled-up to publicly promote and showcase the best version of ourselves – the filtered view we choose to share. Rarely do we see anything but the polar extreme on many platforms. We are all sharing the best of our social lives, holidays, homes, and dinners for all to see. We mostly and conveniently overlook the average or the worst. Rarely do we bear witness to posts about people staying in on their own, not going away, their untidy bedrooms, or disastrous cooking attempts. Like most of us, I am guilty of that.

There isn't enough middle ground in social media land or cloud. This on-screen space is consumed by artificial debate that manipulates and divides opinion. All funded by billionaires and orchestrated by the super-computer wizards of the matrix. On the one side we have the pro-something, with anti-something-else on the other. It stirs up outrage and offence rather than enabling considered and measured discourse. Riots are fuelled, hatred harnessed, and people get hurt and imprisoned. I cannot see a middle ground there at all.

It is the algorithms that are driving us apart. That's what they said in The Social Dilemma, a 2020 American docudrama. We are not all seeing the same things on the internet, our thoughts are tailored and manipulated. We are feeding the central computer with our thoughts and feelings, and behaviours and preferences. A global computer brain storing information, unfailingly remembering it, and manipulating it into thinking for us. It is having our thoughts for us before we have started thinking. It decides what pops up onto our 'phones the moment we reach for them through bleary eyes in the morning. And the spiralling scale is truly mind-blowing. Artificial intelligence? Artificial Machiavellianism!

One quandary with social media is its location, it doesn't really have one, because it is everywhere. The space in which it occupies are its most and least attractive qualities. It is within a virtual world. And in this world, people behave differently than when stood in front of someone, looking directly into their eyes. This is one of the downsides. An unhealthy, damaging and unhelpful side as well. Some platforms are clearly bringing out the worst of our human instincts and urges. They highlight the negative viewpoint or facilitate a bilious diatribe as the target of the day. It really isn't social at all. It is unsocial.

The functionality of social media, and the devices they are on means it can be used anytime, anyplace, anywhere. This means at home and at work, daytime, weekday, weekend, and after 'wine o'clock'. That 'anywhere' can be on the loo, on the bus, in the boardroom, and the bedroom. And if you are a celebrity, a CEO, or politician it has the very real capacity to bypass your agent's best nine-to-five advice, your PR department, or your policy team. There's the risks.

Taking offence.

The engineered and regulated echoes of history still influence what we consciously and unconsciously believe and expect. There are things we can reclaim as good, on the condition we do not unquestionably swallow conventional ethnocentric propaganda, nor its biases. Historical statues, blue plaques, books, films, TV programmes, and music are all obvious symbols in cultural and social subjugation. They show 'posh', straight, male, military, or royal men in impressive uniforms astride horses or atop columns. They have muffled the experiences or diverse voices of those that differ from their norm either by acts of commission or omission – with a few exceptions. These echoes should be catalogued in the library of life, reminding us how far we have travelled (or not) and give us clues as to what future solutions and conscious and positive human behaviours we adopt next.

Progressive dialogue is a positive step change. But some would have it that we also delete the past as it is so offensive and single minded. That's a big concern. We shouldn't submit to cancel culture or erase the past, it tells us too much. On the condition that we keep our reason and nerve and retain a questioning mind and our capacity for free thinking and tolerance. If we wiped out everything that was offensive to anyone, we'd have a very thin cultural footprint to inform today's thinking. We would be devoid of a benchmark, of a measure, of any sense of distance travelled. Our sense of humour may become extinct in due course. Images come to mind of Hitler and pyres of burning books as a prelude to World War II, or of crowds tipping a statue of a slave trader and profiteer, Edward Colston, into the Bristol docks in 2020. Both examples seeking to destroy alternative or past narratives or culture, with admittedly different methods, reasons, scale, intents, and impacts.

It has been really encouraging to see how diverse stories and new perspectives have gradually been given platforms more and more as each year passes, and especially recently. We've seen huge social strides in attitudes and representation of gender, age, religion, sexuality, identity, and race in TV dramas, books, film, and lots of other aspects of popular culture. I'm thinking of things like Black History Month, but there is a danger that some of these things can be approached in tokenistic ways, like tourists people visit briefly and then go back their own lives. Even though there's still much to do, every time we reach a milestone, a new voice is heard. Now is as good a time as any for all people to be listened to and for real change beyond what we have known and what has always been.

Unsocial media.

Social media has given birth to a new species. Trolls. I've had my unfair share of trolling, and one fake account pretending to be me. Given the obvious technological features of online communication, it is somewhat satisfying we use the old term 'troll' to describe those who use it in such inadequate ways. Borrowed from Scandinavian folklore, including Norse mythology over hundreds of years, trolls live in remote rocks, mountains, or caves. Their worlds and family units are small. Having being born and brought up in a small town, I have come to appreciate that small worlds inevitably generate small minds, fear, and prejudices. Trolls are seldom helpful to human beings. Those who troll on social media are people living in small worlds, in 'bedroom caves' or hiding behind screens in the palms of their hands. Absolutely unhelpful to their fellow beings. Shame on them.

The stronger these polarised positions are, the greater the empty space between them. When I have been trolled, the basis of their attack or criticism has invariably been things nothing to do with me. Instead, they have been attributed incorrectly via an unaudited and unchecked trail of content. The social media court of judgement is no more sophisticated than the beach court that tried and hanged that monkey in Hartlepool. But when that happens it sparks a chain reaction of social media commentary and outrage that people adopt as fact. And that is difficult, nay impossible, to correct. Silence is the best defence I have found in these circumstances, which is something that seems to frustrate them much more than a curt and accurate reply.

I've been thinking a lot about social media in my work over the years. Across my day job in early years and especially when starting psychotherapy studies. Mainly because some of what I have seen has not been good. We are being constantly reminded to #bekind and to think about what we say to people online from behind our keyboards or devices. We see again and again the real and dramatic consequences of unthinking and unkind online content. They are unlimited. World wars are traditionally started by the assassination of an archduke, or the invasion of a country. I fear misguided or deliberate social media content could cause the third. It is polarised views, the simplicity of good against evil that are exploited to drive nations to war and to motivate armies of soldiers to fight them. English artist Sir Grayson Perry made the connection between parental violence and war. If a man grows up thinking that violence is a way to solve problems, he may be more open to inflicting this solution on others. The low self-worth of the young man is a social tragedy that makes them think they are on the scrapheap, have little or no prospects, or are cannon fodder. All this must have some connection with this growing willingness to stab each other on the streets for what seem to me to be ever trivial reasons, with the highest possible personal costs. Bringing trauma into family lives through injury, death, and imprisonment.

This is dehumanisation again, the stage four of the steps to genocide, and it forms the conditions for making death threats. How easily these seem to trip off the tongue, or rather the keyboard these days. For the most ridiculously trivial reasons – like missing a penalty. Ask any professional sports player about death threats after missing a goal or costing a match, for example. They are preposterously common, as English psychologist and former professional basketball player John Amaechi showed in his book, Man in the Middle. Thankfully, most of them are just words, they are false threats, but some are not. People go to jail. All of them have emotional effects at all levels. Such attacks are perpetrated and justified by differing viewpoints about a small detail of government policy or guidance. The fall out of England's defeat in the Euro 2020 finals (held in 2021) was only one example. Three Black men in their early twenties, at the top of their game, did their best. They kicked a ball at a goal, and they didn't score. That's all. No one died, but people were threatened with death. If they had scored, they would have been heroes. Instead, they were vilified by an ill-advised minority. The familiar chorus of angry men. Many turned out to be middle aged middle managers - estate agents and the like. It is so depressing, but not surprising. I hope those three young footballers had the support around them and in them to manage such pressures, and for the rest of their careers. And I hope all those perpetrators of hate find peace in themselves or with the love and support of others.

While I have been managing the biggest changes on a national scale, I have noticed the noisy minority, are active, hostile, verbose, and persistent. I've also noticed the quietness, and the silence of the reasonable majority, whose voices are very effectively muffled by the aggression of the louder and dominant dissenting minority. These minority voices are quick to judge and complain and claim to represent the views of the many, but in my view they rarely do, and they certainly don't listen enough nor do the proper research or collect reasonable evidence to prove otherwise. I acknowledge though, that silence can also be a deliberate act of reinforcement, and of agreement, as "anyone who sees inaction in action, and action in inaction, is intelligent..." The Bhagavad Gita, Hindi scripture.

Noise can become louder when people don't feel heard or acknowledged. Anger is fine if it is spent positively and isn't used to cause damage to others. Let go of it and spend it wisely. Turn it into a force for good instead.

Some social media in my professional fields has been unprofessional, disrespectful and unhelpful. It has been immature, cruel, and contradictory. It has not presented our professional roles in the best way, it has not reflected our leadership, tolerance, and commitment to equality. Indeed, in 2024 a UK childminder was jailed for stirring up racial hatred by tweeting that people should attack the hotels housing asylum seekers. They would fail any test against standards of mutual respect and tolerance, democracy, rule of law, and individual liberty. Views and opinions have certainly not been from the middle, they have come from anger and frustration, hatred and abuse.

Freedom of speech cannot include freedom to hate.

In psychotherapy theory, Gutheil & Simon (2005) examined the internet specifically as a 'slippery slope', concluding it had the same capacity for small deviations in boundary crossings to become progressively larger. It's as if once you start, you have lit the metaphorical fuse to an impressive fireworks display. The trouble is it is addictive. People not only like social media. They don't want to let go of it. They are attached to it. I've noticed a real sense of loss if people cannot use it, access it, read it.

Yes, we could all have individual liberty to express our own thoughts in a democracy, for freedom of speech, to lobby, and hold people to account. But language choices, must always be respectful and tolerant of difference. We all have a profound responsibility to be advocates of anti-bullying behaviours that support everyone's self-esteem, wellbeing and personal safety. Freedom of speech cannot include freedom to hate. As Childress and Beauchamp said, we do no harm. The four prima facie principles identified by them in 2001, are a framework for analysing the consequences of our actions. Even though the four principles (respect for autonomy, beneficence, non-maleficence, and justice) were originally applied to bio ethics, they are relevant to many scenarios as they describe them as a 'common morality theory' which relies on 'ordinary shared moral beliefs'. They aim to enhance the interests and happiness of people and of society as a whole. This permits us to develop our own self, as long as it is kind to those around us, is well-intended and is fair. That is our middle moral imperative.

So called 'politically correct' language is important. It isn't nonsense as some would have it, the chosen words are the signs of prejudice and discrimination used constantly and unthinkingly. It is more than an oversight if you think it is trivial, it is a moral responsibility ignored. That's most likely because you haven't been upset, held back, or damaged by these forces. When you know, you notice the smallest, even microscopic things. They are big to us, small to others.

There's body language as well. When you know, you notice the subtleties of prejudice like the merest flick of the eye, tremble of the lip, or change in someone's breathing. These are all much more subtle than funny looks, a raised eyebrow or smile through gritted teeth. You also imagine the unspoken words or the words you expect to be shared once you've left the room, the (dinner) party, or the boardroom. You don't know what people are thinking, but one's experience-fuelled imagination understandably runs wild. When you have a 'characteristic' you always carry the assumptions of others on your back.

Getting on.

Society needn't be so intrinsically partisan or binary – policies could be coproduced. There could be more coalition, more collaboration. Things could be better with applied effort.

I don't always practice what I preach. I remember once I heard a proposed policy, I can't even remember what it was, it was such a long time ago, but I liked it straightaway. That was, until that moment later, when I heard it was the idea of the party I was opposed to. I retracted my support instantly. I was totally and utterly busted. One of those cringeworthy learning experiences. It needn't be like that. But it is. Again, the forces of the narcissism of small differences are in play.

Things need to be much more positive. The culture of party politics usually means you know more about what the politicians are against rather than for. Their criticisms and not their ideas. Their knee-jerk reaction, their DNA, is to decry the policies of the other. What they don't do nearly enough of is develop and share their vision and policies in detail in the middle space. That is until an election campaign when they seek to tempt us, and they try to garner the support of the middle with their shiny new policies and promises. We are instead left with soundbites and bland straplines that appear to be used by everyone interchangeably. Everything, as a result, starts to sound the same. And that only causes us to stop listening and be confused about what to choose.

The middle runs the risk of being an unspoken or overlooked space, one in the shadows, and eclipsed by everything else. And this paints an unnatural picture of what life really is all about. It sets people up to have filtered expectations of their lives. That doesn't seem right to me. This is a terrible oversight, a missed opportunity, a disconnect with so many of our realities.

Media guidelines require balanced representation of views, yet this has constructed a false sense of debate and opinion – it doesn't help much. It requires broadcasters to offer counter views, no matter how extreme it seems. Instead, we could be discussing accepted behaviours and forging confluence, rather than stoking the fires of difference. It only serves to encourage people to stir up false outrage and debate and to think extreme intolerance is more common than it is. But that doesn't make great telly. I am told.

Dawns of realisation.

Recently we have seen change stimulated by high-profile murders, and sexual predations. They have stimulated movements like #blacklivesmatter #reclaimthestreets and #metoo. 2020 was certainly a year of people reacting in various ways to these events, and to consider on a deeper level their reaction and relationship with behaviours, racism and sexism and the terminology associated with all of it. There have been some big challenges for those people who just haven't previously 'got it', don't understand it, and only think of these issues in the most basic or extreme senses. This is a good thing. Not over yet, not a completed piece of work, but there must be some improvement we can celebrate. I despair at the popular press who are too quick to declare the world has changed to such an extent that prejudice is in its death throes. The sad thing is that such developments do push those 'anti' people further back into their trenches of fear and hatred. It polarises our politics and our social media posts. Some become more extreme and revengeful. These are the behaviours of a dying breed. They are pre-extinction bursts where behaviour gets worse before it gets better. Sometimes, people confuse this with the idea we shouldn't stoke the fire, and leave things be instead. Because it would make things worse. That is ill-considered. Progress is hurtful, and it is necessary. A long-term view must be taken.

Technology has to a great extent enabled these movements to be developed and to make an impact. The conviction of George Floyd's murderer in 2021 was abetted by it being captured on a 'phone and distributed on Facebook. A good example of social media being a force for change, so those with privilege are held to account. There's been many such examples since. It seems the mobile 'phone is a new tool of justice and democracy.

Nowadays, workplace misbehaviour is a hot topic in new and different ways. Stories, allegations, and court cases around sexual or behavioural misconduct in the TV and movie industries have generated a lively public debate. We are socially concerned with what acceptable behaviour was in the past and what suitable behaviour is now, and for the future. People have started their careers in one unaccountable culture, and end them, literally, in an accountable one. That can be tough and a shock if you've not kept up with change, or you've not maintained boundaries, or you get caught unawares.

Being reasonable is more interesting than people think.

When you are in the middle, when it comes to opinions, you are deemed reasonable, measured, and balanced in your views. Now I think that is a brilliant place to be. The problem is it just isn't sexy or noticeable enough. No TV producer wants a middle view. They want two polarised views to come together and clash in the name of entertainment of so-called 'balance'. No-one wants to read a balanced review on TripAdvisor – do they? If you are the proprietor, you want to read the gushing positive reviews. Customers, if they want a laugh (or to be shocked) want to read the worst ones.

I wasn't broadcast on the news in an interview about non-essential shops being closed in 2020. I wasn't angry or emotional enough, I wasn't crying or shouting. Those that did were broadcast instead. I was too reasonable. I am happy with that. It is appropriate not to be drawn into such public performances. We can all be more prepared to embrace the average in a glam-sham-social-media-world. Go on I dare you, post on social media that you had beans on toast, stayed in, watched a gardening programme on the TV, and then fell asleep. That's reality.

Taking the middle route through conflict.

As luck would have it, when working on this chapter I ended up in a dispute with a building contractor. I say lucky, only in that it gave me this case study. They caused damage to my office, accepted no liability, believed it was my fault for not advising them of a particular detail. Both sides were firm in their positions. My lawyers and insurers were firmly on our side. What did I do? I stood our ground, but I resisted the temptation for aggression and posturing. I said we wanted to *"find a middle ground and work as promptly as possible to reach a resolution satisfactory to all parties"*. A few emails and some negotiation later and that was exactly what was achieved. That's the way to do it. Taking sides doesn't resolve much. Although their ingratitude was galling.

So, there you have it, the final middle chapter. One that tidied up those common themes and some of the looser ones around the significance of our position and place, and the importance of considering and relating to the people around us. All of this, and the other middles, conflates to drive our behaviour, views, and opinions, our political thinking, and decision-making for the benefit of all of us.

—o—

Be more middle

"If you find yourself stuck in the middle there is only one way to go, forward."

———○———

**Richard Branson,
Businessman.**

As I wrote right at the beginning, this book is all about filling the huge gap left by the lack of useful thinking about all things middle. I invited you to unlearn everything you have been told so far and aim for achieve inner and outer peace, happiness, and joy in the middle.

I hope what you have read has helped you start to rethink and redesign your relationship with your middles. With awareness and understanding we can all reject and reappraise what we have been told. And we can use this to do something much better in our lives or work.

The middle really is an interesting place. It deserves to be better valued and described. The middle merits its own special place in the world, something much more fitting than the current default of being sandwiched between the rest. My mission has been to shed unhelpful attitudes and the deficits of the past and bring the middle into an exciting new and positive space. For now, and for the future.

The middle has a great deal to offer. It can teach us plenty about how to live and work. It can guide us to develop a wonderful perspective and to build an essential skill set of precious qualities, values, and strategies. It is something to aim for, to aspire to, and to value.

Those of you in one or more of the middles, with any luck, are now feeling much more positive about them. Having looked at the five main middles with that very purpose, my wish is that you (and everyone around you) develop an improved and newly rewarding relationship with the middle. A relationship that is more about how we live and work in modern times, and one that recognises all the special qualities, benefits and learning we all gain whilst being there.

There is so much more to the middle than just coping or arriving at confusing and challenging crossroads (and experiencing a so-called crisis). It is much more about robustly realising our own potential, and that of others around us. We can use the middle, and all of its effects, as a powerful force for good. Whether you are interested in societal orders (or class), age, birth order/family position, the middle at work, or occupying the middle ground wherever you are.

Through the journey of this book, I have aimed to regain a real sense of positivity. This could be used to revolutionise how we all describe, live, and work in the middle. And by taking an optimistic and proactive approach, we can all feel much better about it. We can aim for it, be proud in it, and most importantly, find happiness and joy in the middle.

For the middle class – We can all do more to ensure we use class in much more positive ways. This includes detaching ourselves from rigid and archaic categories. Instead, we could be considering ways in which we can all traverse its dangers and prospects. We must avoid any temptation to revel in and reinforce unhelpful differences and divisions. If we do, then all that will be satisfied will be our own self-importance and selfishness. That is not a win. On any measure.

I have outlined why class is still a potent force. It is very much alive and unwell. I wanted to challenge you if you thought there was no such thing as class. If you still hold that view, maybe you re-read that chapter! Class distinction is a pervasive facet, and an instinct of human nature. It saturates all our experiences of social relations, political positions and opinions, connections, and attitudes. As such, class is very powerful indeed. It feeds society's judgement, division, fear, capability to oppress, and fuels social unrest. It magnetises our social groups and fuels our sense of belonging. It permeates politics and the law, social mobility or social control, inequality, and discrimination. Whether these be direct, indirect, or institutionalised. We ignore its forces in our local and global societies at our peril.

Yes, we take heed of the facts and thinking about class, past and present, as such insight helps give us understanding. We can retain the right to self-define and choose our own identities. And that goes for all the other middles, including and especially the **middle age.** We can again take inspiration from Kierkegaard, by not defining or negating, but validating and realising instead.

It is still possible to be aspirational – to be socially and attitudinally mobile – and it is okay. Class and age have become much more fluid than they have been before. We can remain open-minded enough to listen to the perceptions and thoughts of others and engage in constructive and respectful discussion and debate. To reach our happy places. In doing so, we can remember our own experiences and not be in too much of a rush to forget them. Let's develop longer memories please. Using those to invest in our efforts to focus upon what brings us all together and to live more diverse and inclusive lives. I mean, explore, experiment, open up, and skip out of that comfort zone. You'll be surprised how liberating it can be. Look around, are you surrounded by people only like you? If so, it is time for change. There's a big world out there. Where there is difference, this could be valued and respected and understood. Try some new cheese, make some new friends, learn some new things. You might like it. These attitudes all result in a much more peaceful approach to the human condition and is the perfect recipe for social cohesion.

We have learned the middle of life can be a powerful magnet for all sorts of unhelpful humour and for personal identity difficulties. Instead of avoiding or denying it, embrace it I say, it is an all too short-lived moment in our lifetimes, and we can make the absolute most of it. To do that, we must do three things: review, reconcile and reason.

1. Take the time to stop for a moment and review and evaluate your life journey to date. Focus on all the lucky things, the things that are good. Dispel any remembered regrets and cringeworthy moments.

2. In the process, if there is something that doesn't sit well, this needs to be let go. It needs to be reconciled. Loose ends need tidying up, things need to be unlearned or explored in greater detail – with the right support. None of us need to keep hold of anything not useful at this stage, time is too precious, and there is much to get done. Forgive yourself, forgive others. Let go of other people's stuff. This is your life, your rules, your destiny. This is the key to your unlearning. It's your middle after all.

3. Develop a real sense of time and its finitude. We can reason with ourselves, our lives, our careers, and our futures. That is to make sense of it all and to plan, and to put those plans into action. That is the point of planning. And that plan could be a plan for you. it's all possible if there is a plan.

For the middle child – we cannot control our birth or place in the family order. But we can manage what we do with it. The experience of our childhood shapes our adult lives, personalities and characters, ask any psychotherapist or early education practitioner. Its more than a cliché, it is a fact. There is a lot that middle children learn that we can all value and include in our lives and workplaces. If you are one you need to focus on the positives and make informed choices. If you are a sibling, or a parent, or a partner or work colleague of one – the advice is the same. Be positive and exploit their unique talents and perspectives.

There will always be a **middle at work**. It's a fact of work. We can do more to make the middle a better and more vital and successful place. We can lead from the middle. Those working in it need to craft and shape the role to make it their own. And I have given many examples of how this could be done. Middle management is a vital career space, whether you are climbing up or descending the corporate ladder. You are not an inconvenient consequence of organisational growth or structure, nor unnecessary flesh that cost savers can slash away at - you are the bones of the matter.

Everyone can talk about the middle at work a whole lot more and focus on what is important. When we do talk about it, we need to be better. Those unhelpful and blinkered business texts aren't working for the modern workplace. Let's face it, they are authored by Jacks for Jacks, when they really ought to be written by Bernies for Gaylords. It is difficult to change in the middle, granted, but it is not impossible. We can acknowledge these difficulties and barriers and probe them to develop ways to do good things at a successful scale. There are new roles to define here, to be proud of, to be visible in, and to aim for and be happy in. Middle managers need to take up the mantle and be given the chance to fly and become Heads of Being Middle. We could develop all sorts of helpful information and training courses to make this happen, and not be too frightened about it.

Managers and organisations that contain a middle tier really do need to up their game in how they structure, involve, support, and value their middle. Because the middle is the lifeblood of any organisation, it must never be ignored or taken for granted.

For the middle ground, well, there is peace to be had if we reconcile a relationship with the middle. Don't believe the hype, the cutting edge isn't where real change, real harmony, and real impact is made. Quite the opposite. Strong uncompromising direction and dogma only serves to generate a counteraction. The middle place really is the fifth dimension. A space so many cannot see and don't appreciate enough. The middle is a happy space where you can be yourself, exist beyond a false yes-or-no choice. Yes, you will get poked by those around you, just like a middle child, the middle class, the middle age, and those that work in the middle. But we have all found these positions to create a world where peace, love and understanding thrives. It is in the centre where tolerance and movement and change occurs. It really is quite the opposite of being stuck in the middle. We just need to make everyone understand that this is how the world works, and then we might get somewhere.

Adapt and overcome.

The key skill in the middle is the ability to adapt, overcome and grow your own life. To unlearn the unhelpful messages and thinking that came before. To develop self-worth, self-esteem, and self-value. This is easier said than done, but I hope to have been of some use in this book. It does mean being able to change. Including simple things like the type of your jeans, having the confidence to break free of old styles and lifestyles, and choosing new ones that update your look and suit you at the same time. That's actual advice and a metaphor to boot. It also means having the confidence to tailor your social circle or to redraw the boundaries of your relationships, setting out new terms that are more appropriate to how you want to live now and next. It might feel brutal, but any decent gardener will tell you that pruning a woody shrub will most likely promote new growth in the spring. It also includes the capacity to change, grow and develop and remain in your long-term relationship, and not discard that too readily in pursuit of some sort of miracle cure, a panacea to all those things you think are wrong in your life at that point. You might be able to deal with that all on your own, or with your partner, family, or friends. You might just need to take a trusted person shopping with you. Otherwise, it might be time to invest in professional help.

As we know, not enough of us aim for or enjoy the middle. And scant advice, books, route maps, or training appears to be concerned with helping us to get there. Neither is any of that concerned with supporting us when we find ourselves in the middle. You've heard me say that a lot.

It has become abundantly clear to me that the middle position is where we can easily find ourselves. And I think that is a good thing. No, it is a great thing. It is entirely reasonable to accept and enjoy being in the middle. Throughout this book, we have learned about the skills and qualities we can develop when we are there. We have also found the importance of taking into account all of the facts, understanding our self-identity, and benefitting from listening to the views of others we relate with to make sense of the middle. And we have considered the tips and tricks for not just thriving, but surviving, in the middle in the family, in society, and in the workplace.

I started this project when I was approaching middle age at the end of my forties. I was contemplating what was to come and wondering how I would experience this next transition of my life. I came to realise I was in my middle age at the point the book was being finalised as I reached my mid-fifties. My starting position on class was a very strong attachment to my working class roots. Again, I have come to appreciate I am in the technical middle class and have reconciled that so I can best experience the time and place I am in now and for what is to come. These revelations have coincided with my middle age, the sale of my business, and my return (after 25 years away) to working in middle management. Not only was I identifying as all things, but I could also see those around me thought the same of me too. Thank goodness I am ready and prepared. All of this reading, thinking, and writing has been invaluable for me. It gives me great pleasure to share it with you, and I very much hope it will be useful and bring you joy in your middles.

Being middle isn't about being passive or bland. It is about being assertive and vital. And I recommend you to be more middle. Go on, give it a go. The middle is your power base. Be joyful and confident, there is happiness to be had when you know your place and take it with purpose.

—O—

About the author

James Hempsall OBE is a prominent figure in the UK children's services sector. He is the Managing Director of Coram Hempsall's and the National Director for Childcare Works. With over 35 years' experience, he has been instrumental in driving service improvements and leading national implementation of key government programmes in early years and childcare.

He founded Hempsall's in 1999, a consultancy and training organisation that supports early years and childcare providers, local authorities, and government departments. He is a qualified teacher and psychotherapist. Hempsall's work focuses on tackling inequality and improving opportunities for disadvantaged children and families. In 2023, Hempsall's joined the UK's oldest children's charity, The Thomas Coram Foundation Group to become Coram Hempsall's.

James' contributions have been recognised with an OBE for his services to early years education. His leadership and expertise continue to influence policies and practices, ensuring better outcomes for children across the UK. His other interests are in art and design, including being a co-director of Harriman & Co, an independent homeware and furniture store.

References:

Adler, A. (1964) in: Problems of Neurosis: A Book of Case Histories. Mairet P, Editor. New York, NY: Harper & Row, Publishers, Incorporated.

BBC News. Maya Angelou: In her own words. https://www.bbc.co.uk/news/world-us-canada-27610770 28 May 2014. Accessed 05/12/24.

BBC News. Huge survey reveals seven social classes in UK 3 April 2013. https://www.bbc.co.uk/news/uk-22007058 Accessed 15/06/24.

BBC Radio 2. The Liza Tarbuck Show. Broadcast 17 July 2021.

BBC, Sundance TV. State of the Union. 2019-2022. Based on Hornby, N. (2019) State of the Union. Penguin, London.

BBC. The Frost Show. 7 April 1966.

BBC. The Office. Series one, episode six. 2001.

BBC. The Royle Family. Series two, episode one. 1999.

Branson, R. www.quotefancy.com Accessed 05/12/24.

CACI Limited. Do you know your ABC? https://www.caci.co.uk/insights/opinions/do-you-know-your-abc Accessed 07/04/23.

Einstein, A. (1930). What I Believe. Forum and Century.

Freud, S. (2012). A general introduction to psychoanalysis. Wordsworth Editions.

Gould, T. AZQuotes.com Wind and Fly Ltd. 2024.

Gutheil, T. & Simon, R. (2005) Emails, extra-therapeutic contact, and early boundary problems: The internet as a slippery slope. Psychiatric Annals, 35(12), 952-960.

Holocaust Memorial Day Trust. The Ten Stages of Genocide. https://www.hmd.org.uk/learn-about-the-holocaust-and-genocides/what-is-genocide/the-ten-stages-of-genocide/ Accessed 24/10/24.

Ipsos MORI. (June 2016). Highlights June 2016 https://www.ipsos.com/sites/default/files/publication/1970-01/ipsos-research-highlights-june-2016.pdf Accessed 05/12/24.

Jacobs, E. (2015) Identity crisis of the middle manager. Identity crisis of the middle manager | Financial Times Accessed 15/03/21.

Jung, C. (1967) Collected Works 7, Para 114. Routledge and Kegan Paul. UK.

Jung, C. in Perry, G. (2016) The Descent of Man. Penguin, London.

Kochhar, R. (2015). A Global Middle Class Is More Promise than Reality. Pew Research Center. Washington DC.

Kubler Ross, E. (1969). On Death and Dying. The Macmillan Company. New York.

Lennon, J. (1970). Working Class Hero. Signature Box. Apple Records.

Michalowicz, M. (2017). Profit First. Portfolio Penguin. New York.

Mill, J. S. (1859). On Liberty. Penguin, London.

O'Dowd, G. A. (2023). Karma. Bonnier Books, Stockholm.

Office for National Statistics (ONS) National life tables life expectancy in the UK 2020-2022 National life tables life expectancy in the UK 2020 to 2022.pdf Accessed 24/06/24.

Rogers, Everett. (2003). Diffusion of Innovations, 5th Edition. Simon and Schuster. New York.

Ringelmann, M. (1913). Research on animate sources of power: The work of man. Annales de l'Institut National Agronomique.

Salmon, C., Schumann, K. (2011). The Secret Power of Middle Children. Plume Penguin Group. London.

Street-Porter, J. Daily Mail 14 May 2021. https://www.dailymail.co.uk/debate/article-9576531/JANET-STREET-PORTER-Ive-backed-Labour-life-vote-for.html?ito=email_share_article-top Accessed 05/12/24.

Sulloway, F. (1996). Born to Rebel. Pantheon Books. New York.

The Big Bang Theory. CBS. Series one, episode one. 2007.

The Middle. ABC. 2009-2018.

The Muppet Show. ATV, Henson Associates. Series one, episode 110. 7 November 1976.

The Twilight Zone. Paramount. 1959-2020.

Townsend, S. (2012). The Public Confessions of a Middle Aged Woman Aged 55¾. Penguin, London.

UK Government. (2016). British Social Attitudes Survey. https://www.gov.uk/government/statistics/british-social-attitudes-survey-2016 Accessed 05/12/24.

UK Government. (2003). The Victoria Climbie Inquiry: report of an inquiry by Lord Laming.

Winnicott, DW. (1973). The Child, The Family, and the Outside World. Penguin, London.